THOMAS H. OLBRICHT

Life Together

The Heart of Love & Fellowship in I John

dedication

This book is dedicated to Andrew K. Benton, the seventh President of Pepperdine University and presented at the 63rd Annual Bible Lectures, May 2, 2006. President Benton has made a serious commitment to these lectures both in respect to the resources of the University and his own personal time.

Cover design by Rick Gibson
Book design by Mandie Tepe

www.covenantpublishing.com

P.O. Box 390 Webb City, Missouri 64870
Call toll free at 877.673.1015

Library of Congress Cataloging-in-Publication Data
Olbricht, Thomas H.
Life together : the heart of love and fellowship in 1 John / Thomas H. Olbricht.
p. cm.
Includes bibliographical references.
ISBN 1-892435-55-1 (alk. paper)
1. Bible. N.T. Epistle of John. 1st—Criticism, interpretation, etc. 2. Church of Jesus Christ of Latter-day Saints—Doctrines. 3. Mormon Church—Doctrines. I. Title.
BS2805.52.053 2006
227'.9407—dc22

2006009065

TABLE OF *contents*

preface

A jarring incident toward the end of the first century disturbed the churches in Western Asia Minor where John, the aged Apostle, now lived. A number of the members, perhaps some of longer standing, turned their backs on their fellow believers and departed. "They went out from us, but they did not belong to us; for if they had belonged to us, they would have remained with us. But by going out they made it plain that none of them belongs to us" (1 John 2:19). We don't know exactly what these people did when they departed. We do know they were dissatisfied. We know that they disdained the brothers and sisters they left behind. "Those who say, 'I love God,' and hate their brothers and sisters, are liars; for those who do not love a brother or sister whom they have seen, cannot love God whom they have not seen" (1 John 4:20).

Did the dropouts start new churches? We don't know for sure, but it seems likely. Some may have completely drifted away and pursued other interests. Did the defectors claim superiority over the Christians left behind? The secessionists obviously claimed special experiences and insights. They alleged that they were anointed in a special manner, unlike those who remained in these "humdrum" churches. They in turn felt called upon to teach others their superior understandings.

> I write these things to you concerning those who would deceive you. As for you, the anointing that you received from him abides in you, and so you do not need anyone to teach you. But as his anointing teaches you about all things, and is true and is not a

lie, and just as it has taught you, abide in him (1 John 2:26-27).

They also apparently made claims as to sinlessness since John assures those to whom he writes that they can make the same claim. Those who left clearly did not love their brothers and sisters, and in this they sinned despite claiming sinlessness.

> Those who have been born of God do not sin, because God's seed abides in them; they cannot sin, because they have been born of God. The children of God and the children of the devil are revealed in this way: all who do not do what is right are not from God, nor are those who do not love their brothers and sisters (1 John 3:9-10).

Do these calamitous developments strike you as exceptionally unusual? Do they cause you to exclaim, "I never anticipated anything like that would happen in the first-century church!" In all likelihood you will say instead, "It's unfortunate, but I'm not surprised. I know individuals like that. We had people in our church who insisted that they no longer were being fed. They maintained that we only sing those old standard hymns. They feel that instead they have a real need to be lifted up through praise songs. Some of them left our church and went to other churches. A few started meeting in their own homes and anticipated establishing a congregation to their own liking. So I'm not surprised by this turn of events in the first century."

Unfortunately, even from the early days of Christianity people departed from the faithful believers. Jesus anticipated such departures. As his death approached, Jesus implored the disciples, "This is my commandment, that you love one another as I have loved you. No one has greater love than this, to lay down one's life for one's friends" (John 15:12-13). Departures sometimes are the result of alienation from those considered lackadaisical and bogged down with conventions. The people who left the churches in John's circles touted their own superior spirituality. John censured them for leaving. He heralded staying as the appropriate course of action. Those who are superior need to stay around to lift up the timid and the neglectful. Christ himself, though greater than any human by far, vacated his original status and came to live among humans. It is therefore antithetical to being Christ-like to cut loose from those who are inferior in the faith. They are rather to be loved and lifted up. "We know that we have passed from death to life because we love one another. . . We know love by this, that he laid down his life for us—and we ought to lay down our lives for one another" (1 John 3:14, 16).

Some grounds for understanding 1 John will be provided through setting forth what is known about John himself. Other grounds will be laid through exploring the backgrounds of those to whom the letter was written and the situation in which they found themselves.

chapter 1

JOHN, THE AUTHOR OF 1 JOHN

Most biblical scholars from the fourth century to the eighteenth century agreed that John, the son of Zebedee, wrote 1 John, and also authored 2 and 3 John as well as the Gospel and Revelation. This consensus has increasingly eroded since the late seventeen hundreds. But I will not take up the reservations regarding this conclusion at the present. With a wide brush stroke I will first set out the older conventional view.

The New Testament Witness

In the Gospel of John the earliest disciples of Jesus had, prior to meeting him, already attached themselves to John the Baptist. John himself pointed out Jesus to them and identified him as someone special. "Here is the Lamb of God who takes away the sin of the world!" (John 1:29) The next day two of John's disciples were standing with John when Jesus passed by. One of the two was Andrew. After following Jesus to the place where he was staying, Andrew went to find Simon (Peter) told him, "We have found the Messiah" (John 1:41), and then brought him to Jesus. Two other disciples specifically named in the Gospel of John—men who came to Jesus in the early days—are Philip and Nathanael (John 1:43-44).

The second disciple (John 1:40) is unnamed in the Gospel, but early Christian leaders suspected it was John, the son of Zebedee. One reason for this conclusion is that, according to Luke 5:10, James and John partnered with Peter and Andrew in their fishing enterprises. John is never identified by name in the Gospel of John. The sons of Zebedee are mentioned in John 21:2 but not by their names James and John. "The disciple Jesus loved," or "the other disciple," is mentioned several times and by the second century Christian leaders reached the conclusion that "the disciple Jesus loved" was John. In the Gospel of Mark, Jesus first called two fishermen to follow him—Simon (Peter) and Andrew (Mark 1:16). Shortly thereafter Jesus "saw James, son of Zebedee, and his brother John, who were in their boat mending the nets" (Mark 1:19), and he likewise called them. So James and John, the sons of Zebedee, were among the first persons to become disciples of Jesus. Though the author of 1 John is not mentioned in the Epistle itself, sometime in the second century, if not earlier, the author of the letter was declared to be this early fisherman disciple of Jesus, that is, John, the son of Zebedee.

Throughout the Gospels, John, the son of Zebedee, was always paired with his brother James. James and John were in the inner circle of the disciples. Jesus took only Peter, James and John with him when he entered a house to look at Jairus' daughter, who was reported to have died (Mark 5:35-37). Jesus also only invited Peter, James and John to go with him up on the high mountain when he was transfigured before them (Mark 9:2). As Jesus instructed his disciples to prepare for the final Passover meal, he sent Peter and John to orchestrate the arrangements (Luke 22:8). Finally, as Jesus anticipated his death, he withdrew from the other disciples to weep and pray in Gethsemane. Again he took with him only his inner circle of disciples, Peter, James and John (Mark 14:33).

John, the assumed author of 1 John, in these early days apparently stayed in the background, since it was always Peter who spoke up first. Toward the middle of Jesus' ministry, however, John ran into a person who was casting out demons in Jesus' name. Later, in reporting on this incident to Jesus, John was pleased to say that he and others tried to stop the exorcist (Mark 9:38). Jesus responded that they should let the man alone, for "whoever is not against us is for us" (Mark 9:40). Another time when Jesus and the disciples were going to Jerusalem through Samaria, James and John were indignant that the Samaritans denied hospitality to Jesus. "When James and John saw it, they said, 'Lord, do you want us to command fire to come down from heaven and consume them?'" (Luke 9:54). But Jesus rebuked them. It may have been because of their eagerness to incinerate those who resisted that Jesus gave them "the name Boanerges, that is, Sons of Thunder" (Mark 3:17).

James and John at one stage hoped for a privileged position in the kingdom of God that Jesus declared was at hand. They came to Jesus and requested command posts.

> James and John, the sons of Zebedee, came forward to him and said to him, "Teacher, we want you to do for us whatever we ask of you." And he said to them, "What is it you want me to do for you?" And they said to him, "Grant us to sit, one at your right hand and one at your left, in your glory" (Mark 10:35-37).

Their request not only procured the ire of the other disciples (Mark 10:41), but also the reproach of Jesus. He charged James and John with failing to discern the servant nature of his kingdom (Mark 10:43-45).

As the end came, it was John, the disciple Jesus loved, who occupied the privileged place by the side of Jesus during the last supper, taking precedence even over Peter.

> After saying this Jesus was troubled in spirit, and declared, "Very truly, I tell you, one of you will betray me." The disciples looked at one another, uncertain of whom he was speaking. One of his disciples—the one whom Jesus loved—was reclining next to him; Simon Peter therefore motioned to him to ask Jesus of whom he was speaking (John 13:21-24).

It was also the disciple Jesus loved who stood with the women at the cross looking on after all the rest had fled. From the cross Jesus told the disciple he loved, who was standing at the side of Mary, to take care of his mother, and he asked his mother to consider John her son.

> When Jesus saw his mother and the disciple whom he loved stand-

> ing beside her, he said to his mother, "Woman, here is your son." Then he said to the disciple, "Here is your mother." And from that hour the disciple took her into his own home (John 19:26-27).

John therefore, the text suggests, cared for Mary the mother of Jesus from that time on. In Matthew, Mark and Luke, Peter appears to be the premier disciple. In the Gospel of John the exemplary disciple is the one Jesus loved, even though Peter is charged in the end with the task of all the disciples, that is, feeding the sheep.

In the book of Acts, the story of the early church, it is Peter and John among the disciples who take the lead. John now seems to have surpassed his brother James soon after the church was launched on the feast of Pentecost (Acts 2). (In about A. D. 44, Herod Agrippa had James killed with the sword—Acts 12:2). After the day of Pentecost, Peter and John often went to the temple at the time of prayer.

> One day Peter and John were going up to the temple at the hour of prayer, at three o'clock in the afternoon. And a man lame from birth was being carried in. People would lay him daily at the gate of the temple called the Beautiful Gate so that he could ask for alms from those entering the temple. When he saw Peter and John about to go into the temple, he asked them for alms (Acts 3:1-3).

They also proclaimed the death and resurrection of Jesus at the temple, and that resulted in their arrest.

> While Peter and John were speaking to the people, the priests, the captain of the temple, and the Sadducees came to them, much annoyed because they were teaching the people and proclaiming that in Jesus there is the resurrection of the dead. So they arrested them and put them in custody until the next day, for it was already evening (Acts 4:1-3).

It was likewise Peter and John whom the other leaders of the church in Jerusalem sent to Samaria after they heard that Philip had won several Samaritans to Christ.

> Now when the apostles at Jerusalem heard that Samaria had accepted the word of God, they sent Peter and John to them. The two went down and prayed for them that they might receive the Holy Spirit (for as yet the Spirit had not come upon any of them; they had only been baptized in the name of the Lord Jesus). Then Peter and John laid their hands on them, and they received the Holy Spirit (Acts 8:14-17).

Peter and John then spent some time with the Samaritans, speaking "the word of the Lord," and afterward they returned to Jerusalem. John always resided in Jerusalem as far as we know until the city was destroyed in A. D. 70. When Paul went to Jerusalem about A. D. 38, he says James, the brother of the Lord, Peter and John were there:

> When James and Cephas and John, who were acknowledged pillars, recognized the grace that had been given to me, they gave to Barnabas and me the right hand of fellowship, agreeing that we should go to the Gentiles and they to the circumcised (Galatians 2:9).

Paul's cameo description of the Jerusalem leadership provides the last glimpse of John, the son of Zebedee, in the New Testament except, according to the traditional view, in Revelation. "The revelation of Jesus Christ, which God gave him to show his servants what must soon take place; he made it known by sending his angel to his servant John" (Rev. 1:1). When John received this revelation, he was in exile on the Isle of Patmos off the coast of Asia Minor, not far from Ephesus. The common supposition is that the date was about A. D. 95, and John had been involved with a whole series of churches in Asia, as the region was then called.

> I, John, your brother who share with you in Jesus the persecution

> and the kingdom and the patient endurance, was on the island called Patmos because of the word of God and the testimony of Jesus. I was in the spirit on the Lord's day, and I heard behind me a loud voice like a trumpet saying, "Write in a book what you see and send it to the seven churches, to Ephesus, to Smyrna, to Pergamum, to Thyatira, to Sardis, to Philadelphia, and to Laodicea" (Rev. 1:9-11).

From the evidence we have in the New Testament, perceived in the conventional manner, John, the son of Zebedee, was a first-circle disciple, second only to Peter in significance, at least after the resurrection of Jesus. By the time of the conference in Jerusalem (Acts 15), usually dated around A. D. 50, James, the brother of Jesus, emerged as the dominant leader in the Jerusalem church. Peter has his say in the conference (Acts 15:7), but it is James who has the final word (Acts 15:19).

From what we can discover, John stayed in Jerusalem as long as he was permitted. All the Christians left Jerusalem, as did most of the Jews, when it was destroyed in A. D. 70. It is after this date that John, who according to later writers lived longer than any of the other twelve Apostles, worked his way into a leadership role among the growing churches in western Asia Minor. Ultimately, influence of his writings extended into the second-century church and into later Christianity. In the late 40s and 50s A. D., Paul and his converts established churches in Asia Minor. From later documents, especially the history of Eusebius, we learn that John may have been involved in establishing several churches around Ephesus. But the reason John became so influential upon later Christianity was because of the works he wrote, that were conventionally in order, the Gospel of John, 1, 2, and 3 John, and Revelation.

Claims about John in the Historians Writing After the New Testament Period

We now need to back up twenty-five years, go over the events of A. D. 70, and pay attention to what transpired. With the death in 4 B. C. of Herod the Great, the renowned king of Palestine when Christ was born, the region around Jerusalem became a Roman province. Governors appointed by the emperors ruled the province. Because it was a port city, Caesarea (named for the Roman Caesars) replaced Jerusalem as the capital. Jewish laws still prevailed in Palestine, administrated by the high priest and the Sanhedrin, but the ultimate power resided in the provincial Roman governor appointed by the Caesar. Several dissentions existed among the Jews throughout the country, and the governors were often occupied with quelling the rebellions and uprisings.

The famous governor at the time of Jesus' death was Pontius Pilate (A. D. 26-36). Pilate fulfilled his assigned role in many ways but, toward the end, alienated the Jews by setting up gilded shields in Herod's Jerusalem palace. An inscription appeared on the shields naming the person who provided the money as well as the one in whose honor the shield was displayed. Pilate's exhibit antagonized the Jews so much that they complained bitterly, wrote up charges, and had them conveyed to Tiberius Caesar. Infuriated, Tiberius demanded in no uncertain terms that Pilate must remove the shields and transfer them to the provincial headquarters in Caesarea. It was such grievances as this that kept the population unsettled and exasperated the Roman governors.

In A. D. 66 Gessius Florus, who, as it turned out, was the last of the Roman governors in Judea, provoked a Jewish rebellion against the Roman overlords by pilfering funds from the temple treasury. For some time the Jewish military was able to resist the Roman forces sent against them. In the midst of these disturbances, the Christians living in Jerusalem departed for Pella, a city located in the Jordan River Valley about eighteen miles south of the Sea of Galilee. Pella was prominent in the region designated the Decapolis or ten cities that had come under Hellenistic influence. The city was especially prosperous in the middle of the first century. Whether John moved to Pella in the midst of the Jerusalem carnage is not known. Some scholars think that it may have been largely Hellenistic Jewish Christians who relocated there. We know of at least one Hellenistic synagogue in Jerusalem (Acts 6:9), and there may have been more, and there were widows of the Hellenists living in the city (Acts 6:1). So whether John departed with this sizable group that left the city in A. D. 66 is unknown. There are no traditions in that regard. Perhaps many Jewish Christians remained in Jerusalem.

It is most likely, however, that when the Roman soldiers destroyed the city of Jerusalem in A. D. 70, most of the Christians departed. It is known that some Jews remained, including perhaps Jewish Christians, even after the destruction. Traditions preserved by several early church writers declared that John moved to Ephesus, made his home in the city, and that Mary, the mother of Jesus, lived with him. This is said to have transpired because Jesus, as he was upon the cross, requested that the beloved disciple look after his mother (John 19:27).

Over the succeeding months after A. D. 66 the Romans grew more and more provoked over the Jewish resistance, so in A. D. 70 the Roman general Titus was charged by his father, the emperor Vespasian, with destroying the rebellious Jews in the city. Titus later became sole emperor in A. D. 79 at the death of Vespasian. Titus served as emperor jointly with his father up to that point. In A. D. 70, after earlier skirmishes, Titus attacked the city from the north where it was the most vulnerable. In order to prevent goods and people from entering the city, he built a siege wall around Jerusalem, and in due course starvation set in. Josephus described the action.

> The Romans, though it was a terrible struggle to collect the timber, raised their platforms in twenty-one days, having as described before stripped the whole area in a circle round the town to a distance of ten miles. The countryside like the City was a pitiful sight; for where once there had been a lovely vista of woods and parks there was nothing but desert and stumps of trees. No one—not even a foreigner—who had seen the Old Judea and the glorious suburbs of the City, and now set eyes on her present desolation, could have helped sighing and groaning at so terrible a change; for every trace of beauty had been blotted out by war, and nobody who had known it in the past and came upon it suddenly would have recognized the place: when he was already there he would still have been looking for the

City (Flavius Josephus, *The Jewish War*, VI, viii).

The Temple area and the lower city first succumbed to the onslaught. Josephus described it,

> These Romans put the Jews to flight, and proceeded as far as the holy house itself. At which time one of the soldiers, without staying for any orders, and without any concern or dread upon him at so great an undertaking, and being hurried on by a certain divine fury, snatched something out of the materials that were on fire, and being lifted up by another soldier, he set fire to a golden window, through which there was a passage to the rooms that were round about the holy house, on the north side of it. As the flames went upward, the Jews made a great clamour, such as so mighty an affliction required, and ran together to prevent it; and now they spared not their lives any longer, nor suffered anything to restrain their force, since that holy house was perishing . . . thus it was the holy house burnt down . . . Nor can one imagine anything greater or more terrible than this noise; for there was at once a shout of the Roman Legions, who were marching all together, and a sad clamour of the seditious, who were now surrounded with fire and sword . . . the people under a great consternation, made sad moans at the calamity they were under . . . Yet was the misery itself more terrible than this disorder; for one would have thought that the hill itself, on which the Temple stood, was seething hot, as full of fire on every part of it (Josephus, *The Jewish War* VI, iv, 5, 6).

A month later the upper city was taken. Many structures were broken down and burned. The three Herodian towers remained, as did the temple platform and the Jerusalem part of the Western Wall. According to some scholars, Jews continued to worship on the temple mount. It is most likely that whoever among the twelve Apostles were living in Jerusalem at the time of the A. D. 70 destruction fled elsewhere and that

John was among them. The details supplied by the early church historian Eusebius held that John at this time moved to Ephesus and became a leader in the church founded there by Paul about A. D. 55. Eusebius (260-340) wrote his celebrated *Ecclesiastical History* in A. D. 303 and published a final revision in A. D. 325.

Eusebius reported the following regarding the dispersion of the Apostles after the fall of Jerusalem, "Meanwhile the holy apostles and disciples of our Savior were scattered over the whole world. Thomas, tradition tells us, was chosen for Parthia, Andrew for Scythia, John for Asia, where he remained till his death in Ephesus" (III, 1). Eusebius believed that under the reign of Domitian (A. D. 81-96) John was exiled to the Island of Patmos, as declared in Revelation 1:9. At the death of Domitian, John returned and directed the churches in the region about Ephesus (III, 23). Eusebius supported his claims by reference to Irenaeus and Clement. Irenaeus (A. D. 130-200), who grew up in Asia Minor and heard Polycarp (A. D. 69-155) preach, wrote, "And all the elders that associated with John the disciple of the Lord in Asia bear witness that John delivered it [the truth] to them. For he remained among them until the time of Trajan [A. D. 98-117]" (Irenaeus, Book II, *Heresies Answered;* Eusebius III, 23). In Book III of the same work Irenaeus wrote, "The church at Ephesus was founded by Paul, and John remained there till Trajan's time; so she is a true witness to the truth."

Eusebius furthermore observes that Clement, in his work *The Rich Man Who Finds Salvation*, wrote, "And all the elders that associated with John the disciple of the Lord in Asia bear witness that John delivered it [the Gospel] to them. For he remained among them until the time of Trajan" (Eusebius, III, 23). Eusebius declared, in respect to John during the reign of Domitian,

> There is ample evidence that at that time the apostle and evangelist John was still alive, and because of his testimony to the word of God was sentenced to confinement on the island of Patmos (Book III, 18).

RULES FOR HAPPYLIVING

1. **Count your blessings, not your troubles.**
2. **Live one day at a time.**
3. **Learn to say, "I love you."**
4. **Learn to be a giver and not a getter.**
5. **Seek for good in everyone and in everything.**
6. **Pray every day.**
7. **Do at least one good deed each day.**
8. **Learn to count. Get priorities straight.**
9. **Let nothing bother you.**
10. **Practice the "Do it now habit."**
11. **Fill your life with good.**
12. **Learn to laugh and learn to cry.**
13. **Learn to practice the happiness habit.**
14. **Learn to fear nothing or no one.**
15. **Let go and let God take over.**

<u>Climb Happiness Hill</u> by Alan Bryan

"He that will not command his thoughts will soon lose the command of his actions."

ı on Patmos; then later,
n and the three Epistles
was buried in Ephesus,
nartyr and a teacher; he
.e traditional reading of
ment and in the early
:he son of Zebedee, who
leader of a brotherhood
ding 1 John, therefore

›e aware that the older
ıe five Johannine books
ıtion) no longer holds.
ve discussed the author-
ıtroductions to the New
n receive much helpful
th reading, though one
consensus. These recent
ime to understand and
that when one eats baby
ıd stacks the bones on a
: all the recent positions

›f Raymond Brown, the
the Johannine commu-
g 1 John. It is important
t views on authorship to

th century, commenced

ıuthorship see: "Johannine Letters,"
hn H. Hayes (Nashville: Abingdon
k: Doubleday, 1992) III:900-931.

questioning whether John, the son of Zebedee, wrote the Gospel of John. Since we are mostly interested in the Johannine Epistles, however, we will focus on their authorship. Joseph Scalinger (1540-1609), a French Calvinist scholar and later a professor in Geneva and Leiden, wrote that "the three Johannine Epistles are not from the apostle John."[2] His student Hugo Grotius (1583-1645), a Dutch jurist and theologian, rejected John, son of Zebedee, as author of 2 and 3 John and proposed instead as author John the Elder or the Presbyter. (Grotius influenced Alexander Campbell in respect to the biblical dispensations, though not in regard to the authorship of the Epistles of John.) The Elder as author of 2 and 3 John is mentioned in 2:1 and 3:1. Traditionally this elder has been perceived as John the Apostle, since, for example, 1 Peter 5:1 also refers to the author of 1 Peter as an elder. Some scholars have argued that Papias (60-130), who wrote about an Elder John at Ephesus, is describing another John at Ephesus in addition to the apostle. Papias, furthermore, they conclude, ascribes to this other John, the Elder in Ephesus, the authorship of the Gospel and 1 John, and who in turn is the elder (presbyter) of John 2, 3. Oxford professor B. H. Streeter (1874-1937) concluded that the other John, that is, John the Elder, was the author of these documents.

Various later scholars supported the claim regarding John the Elder as author of the Johannine materials, but now only a few critical scholars concur. Most critical scholars are inclined to assign the authorship of the Gospel of John and the Epistles to someone unknown. Even the claim of Oscar Cullmann (1902-1999), a French, Swiss scholar, that the author of the Gospel may have been the beloved disciple—though Lazarus rather than John the Apostle—has received little support.

Doubts regarding John the Apostle as the author of John began systematically with a German scholar, Karl Bretschneider in an 1820 publication. The major German New Testament scholar of the era, F. C. Baur (1792-1860), held the Apostle to be the author of the Gospel, but not of the Epistles. Baur perceived the author of 1 John to be an imitator of John, the son of Zebedee, the author of the Gospel. But throughout the

[2]I'm dependent on Georg Strecker, "Johannine Letters," *DBI*, I:603-609 for some of this detail.

nineteenth century most scholars in Europe and America considered John the Apostle the author of 1 John.

Now, at the end of the twentieth century, few important critical scholars maintain that John the Apostle is the author of 1 John, though the view that the three letters are written by the same author as the Gospel has received renewed support. While some consider the author of 1 John to be a prominent Christian leader from Ephesus, an increasing number are maintaining once again that he is John the Elder (Presbyter) mentioned by Papius. Interestingly enough, however, this authorship is reserved for 1 John, and not 2 and 3 John. The result is that more and more emphasis has been given to the development of a Johannine School in which authorship has been brushed aside for other considerations.

Raymond Brown on the Setting of the Johannine Documents

Raymond Brown proposed four phases in the development of the Johannine community, employing as primary source material the five New Testament books ascribed to John: the Gospel, the three Epistles, and Revelation. He proposed a development in four phases:

1) Origins before the Gospel was written.
2) When the Gospel was written.
3) When the Epistles were written.
4) After the Epistles.

It is of interest to pursue these phases even though this may be unfamiliar territory to those who have read little in recent Johannnine studies. I think the stages he proposes indeed have some basis in the texts, though whether they are as clearly delineated as Brown suggests is a matter that will require far more reflection than we have space for in this book. I think among some scholars there is a propensity to reconstruct a history that is based on a paucity of evidence. Raymond Brown, sometimes I believe, recedes into this category.

Phase One: Origins Before the Gospel Was Written (A. D. 50-90)

Brown believed that the Johannine communities in the beginning consisted of Jews that accepted Jesus as the Messiah, and therefore their origins were not so much in the region around Ephesus but in either Palestine or Antioch. The Johannine churches were, therefore, essentially independent of the churches founded by Paul and constituted by a majority of Gentiles.[3] Brown further observed that the Christology of John is more developed than that of the Synoptics, since the Gospel begins by emphasizing Christ's pre-existence and Messiahship. He further thinks that by the time the Gospel was written the Johannine community was embroiled in a battle with the disciples of John the Baptist, who "claimed that their master was the Messiah or at least the envoy of God" (p. 29). According to the Gospel of John, the first disciples of Jesus came from John the Baptist. The Baptist was therefore incorporated into the Gospel as the one who prepares the way for the Messiah. The beloved disciple, Brown believed, was not one of the twelve but was especially significant, since he gave the Johannine community its independent grounds for being. The beloved disciple in the Gospel, in some measure, upstages Peter (p. 31). The author of 1 John was not the beloved disciple, but he set out to defend the unique Christology of the Gospel of John (p. 31).

Brown believed that the disciples of John the Baptist constituted the earliest persons in the Johannine community, but, as depicted in John 4, a second group entered the picture, that is, those Samaritans converted by the Jewish Christians (p. 37). It is likely that the conversion of a sizable group of Samaritans brought about the earliest "suspicion and hostility of the synagogue leaders" (p. 37). The converts from among the Samaritans rejected the temple and had a high regard for Moses (p. 38). Brown further believed that by the time the Gospel was written, the "Johannine Christians were expelled from the synagogues and were told that the synagogue leaders no longer considered them Jews despite the fact that many were of Jewish ancestry" (p. 41). The synagogue Jews believed that the Johannine community was creating a second God because of what they asserted about Jesus. The Christians' affirmation regarding the divine sta-

[3]Raymond E. Brown, *The Community of the Beloved Disciple: The Life, Loves, and Hates of an Individual Church in the New Testament* (New York: Paulist Press, 1979) 27.

tus of Jesus violated the Deuteronomy injunction that God is one (p. 47). Brown declared that the earliest concentration of the Johannine Christians were Jewish, but he believed that, by the time of the writing of the Gospel, at least in its later stages, a Gentile component now existed because the text explains common Jewish designations such as rabbi (1:38). "We may suspect that it was particularly when the Johannine Christians of Jewish descent were rejected by Judaism and no longer thought of themselves as 'Jews' that they received large numbers of Gentiles into the community" (p. 55). In the first phase the relations of the Johannine believers were with those situated within the Jewish communities. In the second phase, the time at which the Gospel was written, various items within the text are addressed to outsiders.

Phase Two: When the Gospel Was Written (A. D. 90-100)

Brown believed that in the Gospel itself may be found material addressed to three different groups of outsiders that did not believe in Jesus: 1) the world, 2) "the Jews," 3) and the adherents of John the Baptist (p. 62). The "world" rejected the light and hated Jesus and his followers. Jesus overcame the world and drove out the Satanic Prince of the world. The believers at the time of the writing of John were facing Gentile unbelief, as formerly they had faced Jewish unbelief. Jesus was treated as a stranger by the world, and those who believed in him would likewise be viewed as outsiders (p. 64).

The Johannine communities were located in cities and towns in which there were synagogues. The adherents to the synagogues subjected them to persecution. In Revelation a harsh word was spoken about the synagogues at Smyrna and Philadelphia. The location of the seven cities mentioned in Revelation lends support to the conclusion that Ephesus was the center for the Johannine communities (p. 67). Not all Jews at this stage, however, were hostile since some secret believers in Christ still frequented the synagogues. The Gospel of John aims to embolden these reluctant disciples so they will openly confess Christ (p. 68).

In John 3 one reads that disciples of John the Baptist wished to counteract the growing influence of Jesus. In Acts 19 one finds those who were disciples of John the Baptist and who were baptized with John's baptism and had not heard of the Holy Spirit. But this opposition to the disciples of John the Baptist in the Gospel seems less severe than that with the world and with "the Jews" (p. 71).

Brown also believed there were three groups of non-Johannine Christians identifiable in the Gospel: 1) the Crypto-Christian Jews within the synagogues, 2) the Jewish Christian Churches of inadequate faith, and 3) the Christians of the Apostolic churches. Brown bases the existence of Crypto-Christians upon the statement in John 12:42-43 that there were those who believed that Jesus was the Messiah, but they were afraid to declare so publicly for fear they would be expelled from the synagogue (p. 71). For the Gospel writer, Brown thinks, their unwillingness to declare their faith openly was the same as not believing at all. He also concluded that the Gospel of John depicted the Jewish Christian Churches as having inadequate faith. This conclusion was based in part on the declaration that the brothers of Jesus do not believe in him (7:3-5), and that the Jewish Christians are the hirelings who do not protect the sheep against the wolves (10:12). His case, however, it seems to me, is built more on projecting back developments from the second century, developments which in other contexts he advises avoiding. Some in the second century criticized the Jewish Christians for maintaining Jewish predilections such as a low Christology and a separation from the Gentile churches (p. 79). The third category of believers is the Apostolic Churches associated with Peter and the rest of the twelve. The key to the differences the Gospel makes between these churches and the Johannine communities is the manner in which Peter is upstaged on several occasions by the beloved disciple (13:23-26; 18:15-16; 20:2-10; 21:7, 20-24). Brown thinks that the Johannine churches were less interested in ecclesiology than the "apostlic churches," but that they viewed favorably the Apostolic churches (p. 88). He sees the Johannine communities as commanding a unique status, inasmuch as the Paraclete guides these churches, and in this way they are unlike the Apostolic churches. It is difficult, however, to establish two different sets of churches in the region around Ephesus except upon circumstantial evidence. Though admittedly second-century church leaders were interested in placarding unity among the Christians from the first, there is little support for a coterie of churches that had no ties with those founded by Paul and his converts.

Phase Three: When the Epistles Were Written (A. D. 100-110)

We turn now to Phase Three, the focal point for our study of 1 John. Brown held that all three of the Epistles are written by the same person (p. 94), and all come from the same phase of the Johannine churches. He thinks the author is unknown, but in John 2 and 3 the author identifies himself as the elder. Brown grants that in thought and style the Epistles are essentially identical with the Gospel, but he did not believe that 1, 2, 3 John were written by the author of the Gospel, but by a Johannine school of writers (p. 95). The Gospel, he declared, is concerned with outsiders, while the Epistles in contrast are concerned with those formerly within the Johannine churches, that is, the secessionists. As to dates, he concluded that if the Gospel is dated A. D. 90, then "the Epistles might be dated ca. A. D. 100, midway between the Gospel and the writings of Ignatius of Antioch (ca. A. D. 110)" (p. 97).

In regard to the Johannine churches Brown argues that they were not all situated in the same place, since John 2 and 3 were written to churches at a distance and the author was positioned in still yet another location. These churches met in houses, and there may have been several house churches in the same larger town or city. Brown also thinks that other Christian groups may have existed in the same region as declared above. He maintained that the Johannine churches rallied around being taught by the Paraclete. This teaching, which was from the beginning, the beloved disciple passed down. He has passed from the scene but the community keeps his memory alive. Those who pulled out of the mainstream churches were branded secessionists by the author of the Epistles. They held views to which the author objected. The unique features of their views were similar to those Ignatius set out to refute some ten years later (106). Both those who stayed and those who left were grounded in the Christian faith as found in the Gospel of John, but they interpreted it differently. The author of the letters believed that those who left did not appreciate the fundamental teachings of John that the believers proclaimed from their origin (p. 108).

Brown sees the main disputes between those who stayed and those who left centering upon 1) Christology, 2) ethics, 3) eschatology, and 4) pneumatology. Of first importance is the pre-existence of Christ declared in the Gospel and the Epistles. The prominence assigned to Christ's pre-existence tended to overshadow the humanity of Christ. It was because of the claims regarding pre-existence that the Johannine communities were excluded from the synagogue (p. 110). According to Brown, "The Gospel stressed that Jesus is the Son of God; the Epistles stress that Jesus is the Son of God" (p. 111). The opponents so overly emphasize the divine principle in Jesus that they neglect the significance of his earthly career. Are those who left therefore affirming a Docetist view such as that of Cerinthus, who argued that the Christ came upon the man Jesus at the time of his baptism and departed prior to his being nailed on the cross? Brown rejected the position that the secessionists' views were those of or similar to those of Cerinthus on the ground that such could have been easily refuted. I do not find his rejection of Docetic predilections altogether convincing, though I think he is correct in trying to locate the views of the secessionists in the Epistles themselves. I conclude, however, that the statements in the letters make more sense if, in fact, the views of those who left are much the same as those of Cerinthus.

Brown further points out that those who left claimed sinlessness, denigrated keeping the commandments, and by their action exhibited a dearth of brotherly love (p. 123-24). He concluded that the secessionists "gave no salvific importance to ethical behavior" (p. 128). The love commandment in the Johannine writings subsumed all others in respect to the charge against those who left. The secessionists placarded their failure to love by the fact that they withdrew and went their own way (p. 132). Brown argued that those who departed held to a realized eschatology in that they claimed to have attained the ideal relationship with God through Christ. He contended that the author of 1 John did not disagree, but argued that, apart from *koinonia*, the ideal relationship had not in fact been realized. The author declared, "If we walk in the light as he is in the light, we have fellowship with one another" (p. 136).

Brown maintained that the pneumatology of the secessionists was essentially the same as that of the Johannine community. He believes that John addressed pneumatology through Christology. John does not propose a direct means of discerning God's Spirit, rather he focuses on outcomes. Those who affirm that Christ came in the flesh and was identical with Jesus are those who have the Spirit of God. Those who reject this affirmation do not have the Spirit of God (p. 142-44). While Brown's conclusion has merit, nevertheless, the anointing of those who left and those who stayed was to be tested with whether it agreed with that of the author and, in turn, with that of those who remained. The "we" test (1 John 4:6) that "whoever knows God listens to us" has additional ramifications beyond the specific attention given to their inadequate Christology (1 John 4:1-6).

Phase Four: Johannine Dissolution After the Epistles (A. D. 110-)

Brown argues that there is no trace of the Johannine communities in the second century, either of those who remained or those who departed. He thinks the explanation is that those who remained were subsumed into the "Great Church" and the secessionists into Gnosticism (p. 145). This is an interesting admission, since it may also indicate that Brown has overdrawn the independent existence of the Johannine communities from the "Apostolic" churches or Pauline church plants. Since our concern is with 1 John, we will not take up his views as to the specific details.

My summary of Brown's work has not permitted a careful perusal of his conclusions. What I have set out provides the reader with a perspective in regard to what has come to be essentially the critical scholarly consensus with respect to the authorship and audience of 1 John, the requisite data, and why the developments proceeded as they did.

chapter 2

THE JOHANNINE AND THE 1 JOHN PRESUPPOSITIONS

If we agree with the assessment of Brown, the community of believers to whom 1 John is addressed was situated in western Asia in Ephesus and the vicinity around. This circle of churches had developed somewhat independently of the mainstream churches founded by the mission efforts of Paul. While I have doubts about the extent of their independent status, we have benefited from Brown's careful observations. The churches have grown and stabilized for several decades but have now encountered a crisis in which some sizable numbers have withdrawn from the main body of churches. These background circumstances Brown set out are indeed possible even should one contend that John, the son of Zebedee, is the author of the three Epistles. We are now interested in scrutinizing in more detail the basic presuppositions of those who have departed from the older Johannine communities.

The most likely scenario, from my point of view, is that mainstream Johannine thought has been influenced by Hellenistic Jewish outlooks and modes of expression. The secessionists have also been influenced by the same forces but have moved much farther in the direction of religio-speculative Hellenism than those who remain. I conclude, therefore, that those who departed affirmed a vision of God and his universe more inimical to the perspectives of the ones who remained than Brown envisioned. The secessionists embraced a view of reality in which a superior transcendent God has solely indirect influence over an inferior earthly realm but is himself distinctly, wholly other.

Almost fifty years ago my Harvard Divinity School New Testament professor Amos N. Wilder in his *Interpreter's Bible* commentary on the Johannine Epistles wrote,

> In contrast with the Gospel the Epistle has almost no allusion to the Old Testament and lacks evidence of Semitic style. It reflects more directly than John a Hellenistic milieu; see, e. g., the term 'anointing' . . . and the sacramental idea that God's 'seed' . . . makes the believer sinless, as well as the dualism it shares with the Gospel. This Hellenistic background is not Greek, properly speaking, but Oriental-Gnostic. We have sufficient evidence of a religious outlook in the East neither Jewish nor Greek, though influencing both, to which the new faith early accommodated its message in ways quite distinct from Jewish Christianity or Paulinism.[4]

In years prior to Wilder's declaration and afterward, Rudolf Bultmann and several German scholars became proactive in locating an early form of Gnosticism in the outlook of those who left. While I am of the opinion that these German scholars superimposed the more mature Gnosticism of the second century upon the New Testament documents, nevertheless some of the seeds of Gnosticism were already germinating in the first century A. D. Though I do not support the more radical conclusions regarding the influence of Gnosticism on the writings of the New Testament, I think we should not turn our backs completely on such influences, as Brown is inclined to do. Brown was not only interested in avoiding a Gnostic milieu for the Johannnine writings, he declared that scholars should be exceedingly wary of projecting heresies of the second century backward upon these documents and upon the developments in the Johannine communities. I think, however, that Brown set out too

[4]Amos N. Wilder, *The First, Second, and Third Epistles of John* (Nashville: Abingdon Press, 1957) 213.

studiously to avoid these Hellenistic influences, whether Jewish or Gentile, and downplayed some of the more obvious implications of the text as well as the observations regarding this letter by churchmen in the second century.

Now fifty years later, with the discovery of the Qumran documents and their obvious similarity with the Johannine materials in vocabulary and expression, the import of a developed Gnosticism behind these materials has been appreciably reduced. C. Clifton Black has noted these changes in his New Interpreter's Bible commentary on the Letters of John.

> Although the nature of the relationship between John and Qumran remains a debated question, the discovery of the scrolls has indisputably enhanced scholars' appreciation of Jewish influence, beyond the OT, on the Johannine writings. As a result, John's vocabulary and ideas, which at one time seemed closely akin to Greco-Roman mysticism or "higher paganism," have been largely reconceived within the contexts of Palestinian and Hellenistic Judaism.[5]

We need, therefore, to scrutinize views of Hellenized Judaism and of Gentile Hellenism that may inform the outlooks of those who left. Even though we must recognize a much more Jewish milieu for the Johannine documents than was envisioned a century ago, we must not too hurriedly dismiss the possibility that those who left included Gentiles converted from the Hellenists. Robert Kysar, one of the American authorities on the Johannine books, wrote:

> Scholars have often seen a resemblance between this description and the tendencies of "gnostic Christians," who are often called "docetists," because they held that Christ only appeared (Greek, *dokeō*) to be human when in fact he was pure spirit. Furthermore, the group the author describes compares to the "antinomians"

[5]C. Clifton Black, *New Interpreter's Bible* (Nashville: Abingdon Press, 1998) 369.

> among the gnostics who taught that the Christian was free of all moral law—in this case the commandment to love other believers (John 13:34). The author even accuses the opponents of "lawlessness" (3:4). While we do not want to suppose that these dissenters are full-blown gnostic Christians such as arose in the second and third centuries, they appear to have been separatists who held positions which anticipated the emergence of gnostic Christianity.[6]

Kysar went on to cite a study by John Painter, who proposed that "the opponents in 1 John had come into the Johannine community after its break with the synagogue. They were influenced by Hellenistic mystery religions and hence were inclined toward a different interpretation of the Johannine tradition."[7]

I think it is important, first of all, in considering the Hellenistic backgrounds of those who left, to examine the perspective on God, since I believe that it was in their perspective on God that the secessionists basically differed with the leaders in these long developing churches. Because of their doctrine of God, they also had a different prospective on soteriology, Christology, ecclesiology, and ethics.

The First Epistle of John opens by affirming a God who speaks so that humans may hear, who enters into human life in such a manner that he may be seen, and who assimilates into human flesh so that he may be touched. He is a God who enters into *koinonia* with humankind (1 John 1:1-4). He became one with humanity through the entry into the flesh of his Son Jesus Christ. It seems to me that all the pointers in this Epistle suggest that those who have departed affirm a different sort of God, who is so constituted that he cannot make direct contact with material reality. A transcendent God is radically other than materiality.

Ancient Perspectives on God

It would not be unusual if, in the Johannine churches in this time

[6]Robert Kysar, *I, II, III John* (Minneapolis: Augsburg Publishing House, 1986) 17

[7]Ibid., 151 The Painter study is, John Painter, "The 'Opponents' in 1 John," New Testament Studies 32 (1986) 48-71.

and place, some, in fact, did conceive of God as wholly other than humankind—a Deity who is transcendent to the world of contingency and material substance. Plato, Aristotle, Epicurus, and other Greek philosophers affirmed this sort of God, as also did Philo, the Jewish Alexandrian Platonist.

Plato's views on deity are somewhat elusive and perhaps develop over time, if his dialogue *The Timaeus* is one of his last dialogues. It is clear Plato held that there are two levels of reality, an intelligible world and a sense-perceptible world. The intelligible world includes God, perfect ideas or forms, and non-embodied souls. All aspects of the intelligible world are eternal, unchanging, and perfect. They are therefore uncreated. The sense-perceptible world in contrast, as expressed in *The Timaeus*, was not created by God but by a lesser heavenly being identified as the *demiurge*. Since God is eternal and beyond the world's contingency, he does not involve himself with the sense-perceptible world. It is beneath his being and status to do so. The material world is imperfect, changing, and subject to decay and dissolution. Materiality, according to Plutarch (A. D. 45-120), a middle Platonist, is controlled by a "disorderly, 'evil' World Soul."[8]

Aristotle's God, or the prime mover, had a more vital role in the sense-perceptible world by providing it with a constant directed change toward the final cause.

> The prime mover, to satisfy the demands of a remote final cause for all of nature, must be perfect, unchanging, and purely actual . . . [and] may be compared to "pure mind." [9]

Aristotle's Deity, however, likewise had no interest in a personal relationship with the physical world. Brumbaugh declared,

> Since God has no body, and therefore no senses, he cannot know the concrete material individuals of our world. Aristotle consid-

[8]John M. Dillion, "Platonism," *ABD*, 5:379.
[9]Robert S. Brumbaugh, *The Philosophers of Greece* (Albany: State University of New York Press, 1981) 195.

> ers this a sign of excellence. Perishable, accidental things are not worth God's knowing. Divine thought is "thought thinking itself," a baffling description. . . . Aristotle's later comment on the good in nature . . . suggests that perhaps God contemplates the eternal forms in their beautiful systematic interrelationship.[10]

We must be careful not to claim that those in 1 John who departed were well schooled in the ancient Greek philosophers. Nevertheless these same views of deity were propagated by various thinkers in the first century A. D. who were what we might designate popular philosophers. Another case in point is Epicurus and his descendents, the Epicureans. Elizabeth Asmis observed,

> Epicurus thought that it is self-evident that there are gods. But since the universe consists of atoms and void and nothing else, the gods are nothing but complexes of atoms. They live outside any particular world system in the spaces that separate one world from another. Most important, the gods never intervene in the affairs of any world. They do not create or destroy worlds, and they have no concern whatsoever for human beings or anything else in the world. . . . The gods lead a perfectly happy life remote from the world, serving as models of happiness for human beings.[11]

Though the main influence of the Epicureans was before the first century A. D., some were still around in the early days of Christianity. Lucretius, who wrote his famous treatise "On the Nature of the Universe," lived in the prior century. Philo opposed Epicurus' hedonism and denial of providence. In Acts 17:18, Epicureans are declared to be critics of Paul. Clearly, therefore, Hellenism supplied the roots for belief in a God who was so wholly other that he by his very nature could not function in an inferior sense world.

[10]*Ibid.*
[11]Elizabeth Asmis, "Epicureanism," *ABD*, 2:560.

spirit that confesses that Jesus Christ has come in the flesh is from God, and every spirit that does not confess Jesus is not from God" (1 John 4:2-3). In other words, there are those who confess that the suprasensible Christ inhabited Jesus, but that Jesus the man was not, as such, the Christ. God himself, as well as his Son, the Christ, because of their very nature negated a genuine rapprochement with the flesh. The Spirit is superior to the flesh. For this reason those who are spiritually discerning are justified in turning their backs on those spiritually inferior. It is quite proper for them to go out from among those who are a reproach to true spirituality (1 John 2:19)!

In another one hundred years after 1 John was written such people had become full-blown Gnostics. By the time the Epistle was written they had not yet became a significant schism in Christianity. There were, in fact, many varieties of Gnostics in the second century. A common belief among them, however, was that God was transcendent and abhorred physical reality. Edwin M. Yamauchi observed,

> Because there was no central authority or canon of scriptures, the Gnostics taught a bewildering variety of views. Fundamental to clearly gnostic systems was a dualism that opposed the transcendent God and an ignorant demiurge (often a caricature of the OT Jehovah). In some systems the creation of the world resulted from the presumption of Sophia (Wisdom). The material creation, including the body, was regarded as inherently evil. Sparks of divinity, however, had been encapsuled in the bodies of certain pneumatic or spiritual individuals, who were ignorant of their celestial origins. The transcendent God sent down a redeemer, who brought them salvation in the form of secret gnosis. Gnostics hoped to escape from the prison of their bodies at death and to traverse planetary spheres of hostile demons to be reunited with God. There was for them, of course, no reason to believe in the resurrection of the body.[15]

[15]Edwin M. Yamauchi, "Gnosticism," *Dictionary of New Testament Background*, eds. Craig A. Evans & Stanley E. Porter (Downers Grove: InterVarsity Press, 2000) 416.

The people who left the Johannine communities were not mature Gnostics, but they were on the way.

In the meantime, it seems to me that Cerinthus, as early church historians maintained, held views of the sort that were at least similar to those of the separatists. Cerinthus lived in Asia Minor about A. D. 100. According to Irenaeus, John wrote his Gospel against the teaching of Cerinthus.[16] In the Christology of Cerinthus, according to Hippolytus, Christ occupied the human Jesus but did not fully assimilate into his humanity, since to do so would be foreign to the very nature of God. About the views of Cerinthus, Hippolytus wrote:

> But a certain Cerinthus, himself being disciplined in the teaching of the Egyptians, asserted that the world was not made by the primal Deity, but by some virtue which was an offshoot from that Power which is above all things, and which (yet) is ignorant of the God that is above all. And he supposed that Jesus was not generated from a virgin, but that he was born son of Joseph and Mary, just in a manner similar with the rest of men, and that (Jesus) was more just and more wise (than all the human race). And (Cerinthus alleges) that, after the baptism (of our Lord), Christ in form of a dove came down upon him, from that absolute sovereignty which is above all things. And then, (according to this heretic,) Jesus proceeded to preach the unknown Father, and in attestation (of his mission) to work miracles. It was, however, (the opinion of Cerinthus) that ultimately Christ departed from Jesus, and that Jesus suffered and rose again; whereas that Christ, being spiritual, remained beyond the possibility of suffering.[17]

Though scholars in the twentieth century have been reluctant to consider 1 John as an effort to confront the views of Cerinthus or views

[16]Irenaeus, *Adv. Haeres*, 3.11.1.
[17]Hippolytus, *Refutation of All Heresies*, VII, 21.

similar to his, it seems to me that these perspectives best explain statements in the letter. I will show in my comments on the text that much in the letter may be explained from the standpoint that those who left held a view of God and Christ that perceived Deity as constitutionally unable to enter into the sensed world of material. For that reason, those who perceived God and Christ aright, according to the claims of the secessionists, were fully justified in withdrawing from spiritually inferior brothers and sisters who had not yet come to a conviction of God's wholly other transcendental nature.

The Purpose and Message of 1 John

Commentators hold more diverse perspectives on 1 John than on perhaps any other book in Scripture. I believe that 1 John was written to the members of the churches in the region around Ephesus, perhaps including the seven churches of Asia (Revelation 2, 3). It was written after the Gospel of John. A crisis arose in these churches because of certain members who left (1 John 2:18-19). Those departing claimed special insights regarding God and Christ as well as maintaining that they exercised a superior purity of life. John wrote this letter, not so much to denounce and call to repentance the defectors, but to bolster those who remained. Rather than retrenching into an inferiority complex, the loyal should exhibit the utmost confidence in the original message they received. "Let what you heard from the beginning abide in you. If what you heard from the beginning abides in you, then you will abide in the Son and in the Father. And this is what he has promised us, eternal life" (1 John 2:24-25).

The rhetoric or persuasion in 1 John can therefore be designated "continuational." In this regard the exhortation of 1 John is similar to that of Colossians.[18] All the remarks in 1 John, it appears to me, are designed to restore the confidence of the believers who remain in respect to the views they hold and the life they live. They are to abide in what they

[18]Thomas H. Olbricht, "The Rhetoric of Colossians," *Rhetoric, Theology and the Scriptures, The Pretoria Conference, 1994*, Stanley E. Porter and Thomas H. Olbricht, eds. (Sheffield: The University of Sheffield Press, 1995) 308-328.

believed and lived from the beginning. They are to affirm a God who was in fellowship with his Son. His Son was in turn in fellowship with the disciples, and the disciples in fellowship with those who responded to the Gospel. Those who accepted Jesus as the Christ are in turn to be in fellowship with God, Christ, the Apostles, and with each other.

Paul wrote Colossians with a similar purpose. "As you therefore have received Christ Jesus the Lord, continue to live your lives in him, rooted and built up in him and established in the faith, just as you were taught, abounding in thanksgiving" (Col. 2:6-7). Paul feared that certain Colossians might drift away because they were on the verge of accepting numerous heavenly beings as of equal importance with the Lord Jesus Christ. They were apparently tempted to worship angelic beings. They also contemplated embracing detailed observances that augmented, so they thought, a superior lifestyle.

We live in an era in which church members are desperately in need of the challenge from 1 John to stay the course. Modern revised versions of the Christian faith are constantly bombarding believers. Popular media proclaimers herald miscellaneous species of revisionism. New theologies and practices may be found in religious publications and on Internet lists. Multitudinous perspectives are being passed along by word of mouth from church acquaintances, friends, and relatives. Believers who remain loyal to earlier views are labeled as mossbacks or reactionaries. Recent trends are sometimes of value, but not automatically. Before believers consider moving on, both Paul and John challenge them to reflect upon and relish the earlier perspectives by which they entered the faith. Constancy in staying the course is recommended to others both in appreciating the forefathers and in remaining in place.

1 John was written after Christianity had spread from Jerusalem, then to all of Judea, to Samaria, and to the uttermost parts of the world (Acts 1:7-8). By the time 1 John was written, Christianity had acquired numerous adherents in Asia Minor with Ephesus being a center for Christian evangelism and learning. By A. D. 90 the majority of Christians lived in that region. In A. D. 70 Jerusalem was destroyed and those of Jewish heritage, both traditional Jews and Christians migrated elsewhere. This is, as

I see it, an accurate statement, though a few may have remained. Paul and those he converted were the first to take the gospel to many of the key cities in Asia Minor. John migrated there after the fall of Jerusalem, and he too contributed to the growing churches and their understanding of faith in Jesus as the Messiah of God. W. H. C. Frend wrote,

> The province of Asia emerged as the area where Christianity was strongest, with Ephesus as its radial point. Ephesus is the first of seven churches addressed by the Seer of Patmos and it was the provincial capital of Asia. This was where one would have sought the Gnostic heretic Cerinthus as well as Paul's successors.[19]

Much like the United States in the twenty-first century, Asia Minor in the first century contained major strains of philosophical and religious outlooks. If diversity in a region is a boon, Asia Minor had diversity!

Already by the time 1 John was written, revisionist Christian leaders promoted the advance of new versions of the Christian faith. Jewish leaders in Asia Minor had been hellenized for some time, and it is not surprising that Christianity rather early incorporated and tolerated hellenization. The backgrounds of the new believers who soon became teachers were often Platonistic, while still others reflected native religious views disseminated in the region. These modified views have entered the Johannine churches and are threatening their stability. By the time John wrote 1 John, those who left had embraced some sort of hellenized theology and, hence, Christology. One might argue that their departure was one of the best things that could have happened to the churches. But it is clear John thought that their departure left an aura of uncertainty in its wake. Those who left chided the ones who remained as having an inferior understanding as well as a sluggish religious commitment. Rensberger appropriately observed,

> The opponents' position was probably affected by the dualism of

[19]W. H. C. Frend, *The Rise of Christianity* (Philadelphia: Fortress Press, 1984) 127.

> hellenistic culture, and therefore it presents an early instance of a perpetual problem in Christian mission, the extent to which the presentation of the gospel can be adapted to local cultures. The hellenism of the eastern Mediterranean was one such local culture, and the New Testament writings exemplify in various ways both adaptation to it (most notably the Gospel of John itself) and critique of adaptations considered too extreme (e.g., 2 Corinthians and Colossians). The opponents may have thought that their numerical success confirmed the validity and divine inspiration of their christological message. Our author feared that they were in danger of losing the truly Christian character of the gospel altogether. The point he makes is that if those who hear the message are of God, they will listen to the gospel of the Incarnation. It is not open to the evangelist to sugarcoat the message with a popular spirituality that might cut it loose from the contingent and everyday nature—the flesh—of human life, both Jesus' and our own.[20]

Those Hellenists of a philosophical bent conceived of God as essentially uninvolved in the lives of humankind. He was a deity who transcended all that is corporeal. He lived in a suprasensible realm untouched by the affairs of the material world. For both Plato and Aristotle the physical universe is eternal. Deity did not create the universe; it has always existed. In more popular versions of ancient myths, the universe in some manner produced the panoply of gods. Humans, too, were not created by deity in the thought of Plato, or at least, by the singular god. The souls of humans, according to Plato, have always existed and will always exist—they are immortal. Souls are reincarnated not only as human beings, but also as birds and animals. In *The Timaeus* Plato apparently entertained the prospect that a lesser deity, the demiurge, commissioned by God, created the universe.

Aristotle believed that the universe is infinite in space and time. He

[20]David Rensberger, *1 John, 2 John, 3 John*, 115.

believed that deity supplies motion to the universe, but simultaneously, so that both God and the universe have always existed. He believed that the deity was not involved in human life but that God spent his time in the highest form of existence, that is, contemplation, and in the case of God it was self-contemplation. The souls of humans have always existed as a grand deposit of "soulness" in the universe. But when humans die, the active mind returns to the pool of minds, and from that pool a mind enters another physical human. The souls or active minds are therefore immortal, but there is no such thing as individual immortality.

From the filtered-down views of these earlier philosophers, the intellectuals of John's era believed in one God who was above time and space and uninvolved in any manner with humankind or the physical universe. More popular philosophers believed that God, or the gods, might visit the earth, and perhaps even dwell in biological humans. Nevertheless the deity was always hermetically sealed off from the physical of humans and their flesh. God is not someone to be seen, heard, or touched, according to the popular philosophers, neither among the Jews nor the original inhabitants of Asia Minor.

The chief witness of the Scriptures is that God (Genesis 1) created the universe and also humans. In fact, humans are created in the image of God (Genesis 1, 2). The God of Scriptures continually reached out to humanity. He appeared to Abraham and promised to bless him and through his descendents to bless the nations of the world. He repeated the promise to Isaac and Jacob. God revealed his will for his people on the mountain as he itemized the law to Moses. He was present with David through his many battles and promised him a forever dynasty. He proposed to Solomon that he ask for a gift. When Solomon asked for wisdom to rule God's people judiciously, God praised his decision and declared also that he would become wealthy and live a long life. God sent his word to his people through several prophets and, in fact, one declared, "Surely the Lord God does nothing, without revealing his secret to his servants the prophets." (Amos 3:7). And finally, according to John, God revealed himself in a special manner through his Son. "No one has ever seen God. It is God the only Son, who is close to the Father's heart, who has made him known" (John 1:18). The Son did not disdain material and biological existence but freely disseminated himself bodily within the physical world. "And the Word became flesh and lived among us, and we have seen his glory, the glory as of a father's only son, full of grace and truth" (John 1:14).

It is not fully clear just in what sense those who left the Johannine communities declared God inimical to the world of physical matter. But it is certain that John highlighted the God who appeared to Abraham, Isaac, and Jacob, a God who so loved the world that he sent his only Son to be born of woman. We do know the separatists declared that the Christ inhabited Jesus, rather than that the man Jesus was in himself the Christ. I think it is likely that they held a view much similar to that of Cerinthus in which the Christ came upon Jesus at the baptism and departed prior to his death on the cross. In that manner God dwelt within a human but was hermetically sealed off from human flesh. John clearly countered such a view. "By this you know the Spirit of God: every spirit that confesses that Jesus Christ has come in the flesh is from God, and every spirit that does not confess Jesus is not from God" (1 John 4:2-3). Those who departed believed that their understanding of God did not come through the channels of the regular teaching and preaching that brought them into the Christian faith but through a specially revealed private message. They were also God's special people because of a special private anointment.

Because of their perspectives on God, those who left also concluded that it was entirely appropriate to separate themselves from those beneath them spiritually. John chides them by declaring that those who love God also love his children.

Those who say, "I love God," and hate their brothers or sisters, are liars; for those who do not love a brother or sister whom they have seen, cannot love God whom they have not seen. The commandment we have from him is this: those who love God must love their brothers and sisters also (1 John 4:20-21).

Those who left claimed perfection because of their special knowledge (gnosis) and anointment. They apparently claimed to maintain a rigorous moral perfection, since John declared, "If we say that we have not sinned, we make him a liar, and his word is not in us" (1 John 1:10).

In the twenty-first century, deviant Christian groups still profess that God is above and beyond the physical and does not enter into it in any manner. He is a God who cannot be touched, seen, nor, in fact, heard. What is heard among certain Charismatics is that the Holy Spirit not only speaks but also empowers special servants of God to perform uncommon feats of healing and prophecies. Not only is God withdrawn and remote, so also is his human manifestation in a man. Jesus is not the Son of God. He is the perfect man. Jesus is to be admired and respected, but the direct contact of the believer with God is through the Holy Spirit. Only the Holy Spirit is accessible and involved with the life of humankind.

The message of John in his Epistle is that God himself has permitted humans to see, hear, and touch his very being. The God of the universe has entered human flesh and made it possible for biological, material humans to take up a new existence through fellowship with him, his Son, the Son's first disciples, and with other believers. "If we walk in the light as he himself is in the light, we have fellowship with one another, and the blood of Jesus his son cleanses us from all sin" (1 John 1:7).

The God who appeared to Abraham, Isaac, and Jacob was a God who wished to make his presence known. He is a God who is best known through his mighty acts publicly exhibited.

Samuel said to the people, "The Lord is witness, who appointed Moses and Aaron and brought your ancestors up out of the land of Egypt. Now therefore take your stand, so that I may enter into judgment with you before the Lord, and I will declare to you all the saving deeds of the Lord that he performed for you and for your ancestors" (1 Samuel 12:6-7).

There are several catalogs of the mighty acts of God in the Old Testament (for example, Deuteronomy 26; Psalms 105, 106, 136; Nehemiah 9). A shorter version is,

Psalm 135:6-12

Whatever the Lord pleases he does,
in heaven and on earth,
in the seas and all deeps.

He it is who makes the clouds rise at the end of the earth;
he makes lightnings for the rain
and brings out the wind from his storehouses.
He it was who struck down the firstborn of Egypt,
both human beings and animals;
he sent signs and wonders
into your midst, O Egypt,
against Pharaoh and all his servants.
He struck down many nations
and killed mighty kings—
Sihon, king of the Amorites,
and Og, king of Bashan,
and all the kingdoms of Canaan—
and gave their land as a heritage,
a heritage to his people Israel.

The Father of our Lord Jesus Christ does not reveal himself in special mysterious knowledge. He does not reveal himself in special ecstatic experiences. He is a God who concretely manifested himself in the flesh so that he could be heard, seen, and touched.

chapter 3

THE KOINONIA OF GOD
1 John 1:1-7

The Prologue—1 John 1:1-4

1 John commences with a prologue just as does the Gospel. Why doesn't 1 John start like an Epistle with greetings and comments on the recipients and their location? Because of the absence of a normal epistolary introduction, some scholars think that "treatise" is a more appropriate appellation for 1 John than "epistle." D. Moody Smith's observations are apropos.

> It may well be that 1 John lacks an epistolary opening precisely in order to evoke the Gospel. Instead of a greeting we find a prologue. By emulating the form of the Gospel's prologue, the writer immediately calls the reader's attention to the importance of the relationship of what he is writing to the Gospel.[21]

We will do well, however, to discern the reason for the specific prologue to 1 John. Admittedly, there are several similarities of the prologue of the Gospel in vocabulary and conceptions with that of the Epistle. But the purposes of the two differ. I have already argued that 1 John commences with declarations regarding the tangible manner in which God

[21]D. Moody Smith, *First, Second, and Third John* (Louisville: John Knox, 1991) 35.

has disclosed himself through the Son. John commences in this manner because those who left conceive God as transcendent and unavailable to enfleshed humans. John maintains that God is *koinonia*. He is not, as those who left perceived, unable to enter into a relationship with the creatures of a material world and therefore antithetical to them.

This is not to say, however, that John proceeds with a head-on attack and refutation of the secessionists. Had he done so, we could be more confident of what their views actually were. Rather, and I suggest, wisely, he opposed what he considered their erroneous views on God through a detailed and powerful setting forth of the correct views.

The prologue of the Gospel focuses upon the Word in his relationship with God, but then also with humankind. The prologue to 1 John focuses upon the Father and the Son in their relationship with those who have come to faith. In both cases God is one who enters fully into the very life and being of humans. In the Gospel, the Word "became flesh and lived among us, and we have seen his glory" (John 1:14). In 1 John, God is the one who enters into the world of corporeal humanity so that he may be heard, seen, and touched. It is the latter that apparently those who left denied. John has not written this discourse to win them back. Rather, he has written it to bolster the conviction of those who stayed that what they learned from the beginning was the indisputable truth. It is an authentic apostolic view of God with its various ramifications that must sustain and inform the community of faith.

In 1:1 the author starts out with a Greek construction that implies the use of we. "We" may be editorial. A more common perception, however, is that the author is writing on behalf of a community of churches and that he is speaking for the community.[22] Should the author be John the Apostle, then he is no doubt making reference to the experiences of the twelve with Jesus. The "we" of 1 John 4:6, therefore, would have in mind the apostolic witness which, according to John, forms the basis for distinguishing the authentic teaching from that which is spurious. "We are from God. Whoever knows God listens to us, and whoever is not from

[22]Robert Kysar, *I, II, III*, 32.

God does not listen to us" (1John 4:6).

The next phrase "what was from the beginning" also requires explanation. The statement reminds us of "In the beginning was the Word" (John 1:1). Is this then a declaration about the advent of the Word and his proclamation in the Johannine community, or is it an express attempt to declare the pre-existence of Jesus the Son? I think there is no question but that the pre-existence of Jesus is presumed in 1 John, but "from the beginning" more likely points to the beginning of Jesus' appearance on earth, that is, his incarnation and the proclamation of that appearance. It was at that time that Jesus made it possible to hear, see, and touch God. It is this same meaning found in 1 John 2:7, 24; 3:11; and also 2 John 5-6. Rudolf Snackenburg commented,

> The phrase "from the beginning," frequently used in 1 John, refers for the most part to the doctrine proclaimed at the beginning and is intended to move the readers to remain faithful to that doctrine as against the teachers of heresy who appeared only later. But there is a more profound, substantial reason for this early Christian principle of tradition. The message proclaimed "from the beginning" also includes the personal bearer of an archetypal Being ("him who is from the beginning," 2:13-14).[23]

The claim of the author unmistakably implies that he himself heard, saw, and touched the "word of life," who is clearly the Son, Jesus Christ (1:3). Commentators who do not believe that John the Apostle is the author claim that the statement implies not a firsthand witness to the Son, but rather to the message that was received from prior witnesses.[24] Houlden wrote,

> It is more probable that he consciously takes the mantle of orthodoxy: he speaks for and is at one with all those who have

[23]Rudolf Schnackenburg, *The Johannine Epistles: Introduction and Commentary* (New York: Crossroad, 1992) 57.
[24]*Ibid.*, 52.

> thought rightly about Jesus from the beginning—and that of course includes those who first saw, heard and felt. He identifies himself with them. . . .[25]

Regarding hearing and seeing, Houlden's explanation is possible. But when the author alleges "touched with our hands," the clear implication seems to be that he and others were actually in the presence of Jesus and touched him.

What the author and others apprehended concretely is the word of life, and that life is eternal (1:3). The word of life, that is, the eternal life was with the Father. Though the text does not so declare, the inference is that the Son and the Father shared eternal life. They were involved in *koinonia.* John in this first letter focuses upon *koinonia.* The life of the believer in Jesus Christ consists of fellowship (*koinonia* in the Greek), both because the crucial attribute of God is *koinonia,* and because those who likewise love God must replicate his *koinonia* in the body of believers.

In the theology of John, God is the one who reaches out in fellowship to the universe he has created and especially to the humans made in his image. He has done this in a new and unique manner through the "word of life" (1 John 1:1)—a word of life heard, seen, and touched and revealed. The Father and the "word of life" shared eternal life (1 John 1:2) and then revealed it to those first believers who saw and heard. So the first believers were likewise incorporated into eternal life because they shared *koinonia* with "the Father and with his Son Jesus Christ" (1 John 1:3). The "word of life" is therefore the Word who was in the beginning with God and was God (John 1:1)—Jesus Christ, the only begotten Son of God (John 3:16). God himself does not hold his creation at arms' length. Rather, he embraces it. The fundamental essence of God is *koinonia.* God is a God who seeks fellowship.

The first believers were drawn into the *koinonia* with God through the "word of life." They, in turn, that is, the disciples, reached out to extend this *koinonia* to others, "so that you also may have fellowship with

[25] J. L. Houlden, *The Johannine Epistles* (New York: Harper & Row, 1973) 53.

us" (1 John 1:3). Not only do the believers to whom this letter was written have fellowship with God, they also have fellowship with one another. "But if we walk in the light as he himself is in the light, we have fellowship with one another" (1 John 1:7). They become communities of faith strongly bonded in love. "God is love, and those who abide in love abide in God, and God abides in them. Love has been perfected among us in this" (1 John 4:16-17). The *koinonia* and agape of God and his Son are the fountainheads of fellowship in 1 John.

1 John is written because of secessionists who denied that God reaches out to embrace the world. They believed that God seals off himself hermetically from the material world, since God by his very nature transcends all that is physical and biological. He is a stand-apart deity! He cannot be seen, heard, or touched. He is the wholly other God. From the standpoint of John, the God who holds himself apart is not the God who revealed himself to Abraham, Isaac, and Jacob. Declarations concerning a wholly other God for John are bad theology. John expresses his own interest in extending *koinonia* to all who will receive it by declaring that in writing about the divine *koinonia* he is completing his joy. "We are writing these things so that our joy may be complete" (1 John 1:4).

The Fellowship of God and the Fellowship of the Believers—1 John 1:5-7

God is depicted as light. "God is light and in him there is no darkness at all" (1 John 1:5). One is reminded of the Gospel. It is Jesus in the Gospel, however, rather than God who is declared to be the light and contrasted with darkness. "As long as I am in the world, I am the light of the world" (John 9:5). "Again Jesus spoke to them, saying, 'I am the light of the world. Whoever follows me will never walk in darkness but will have the light of life'" (John 8:12). The question now occurs, in what sense is God the light? I think that since the emphasis on fellowship precedes the statement about light and reoccurs again following the statement about the light of God, we must say that the light of God is his *koinonia*. God in his very being reaches out to the world and to the creatures he has brought forth. His reaching out defines who he is. *Koinonia* is the light of God.

The implication of God as light for the believers is that they must be light in the same sense. God is faithful in fellowship. The believer who walks in the light walks in fellowship. Pheme Perkins has pointed out that the view of Jesus and God as light is not an inner illumination or internal guide to goodness.

> When applied to Jesus in the gospel, light imagery symbolized his revelation as saving humanity. Applied to the Father, here, it symbolizes the perfection and purity of his divinity. But unlike many forms of hellenistic and gnostic piety, association of light with divine being did not mean that people were to seek a personal, private, interior vision of that divine light. It meant, as the author will go on to spell out, that they were to conduct their lives in obedience and fidelity to the community which that God had acted to establish (1:6f; 2:10f).[26]

In the past I heard sermons in which it was maintained that walking in the light of God means to embrace and affirm the doctrine found in the New Testament. The proclaimer of the word must declare the teachings of God. Often the statement of 1 Peter was quoted.

> If any man speak, let him speak as the oracles of God; if any man minister, let him do it as of the ability which God giveth: that God in all things may be glorified through Jesus Christ, to whom be praise and dominion for ever and ever. Amen (1 Peter 4:11, KJV).

Furthermore, all the words of God inscripturated are worthy.

> All scripture is inspired by God and is useful for teaching, for reproof, for correction, and for training in righteousness, so that everyone who belongs to God may be proficient, equipped for

[26]Pheme Perkins, *The Johannine Epistles* (Wilmington: Michael Glazier Inc., 1997) 16.

every good work (2 Timothy 3:16-17).

The preachers upon this basis proclaimed that those who walked in the light of God declared and embraced the whole doctrine of God. Whatever merit there may be in what the preachers maintained, and certainly the sermons had a good biblical point, that is not what walking in the light of God means in 1 John 1:7. To walk in the light of God in this text clearly means to engage in fellowship (*koinonia*) just as God engages in fellowship.

Walking in darkness, contrariwise, is to walk by oneself or with a limited group of associates. "Whoever says, 'I am in the light,' while hating a brother or sister, is still in the darkness" (1 John 2:9). "But whoever hates another believer is in the darkness, walks in the darkness, and does not know the way to go, because the darkness has brought on blindness" (1 John 2:11). There is no darkness at all in God because he constantly reaches out in fellowship to what he has made. Those who refrain from fellowship are in darkness. The one who presumes to walk with God must walk as he walks, that is, with others. Those who withdraw and no longer walk with their fellow believers are walking in darkness. If they say they have fellowship with God, yet persist in erecting walls with their brothers and sisters, they are not walking with God. They are not speaking the truth, but lying. "If we say that we have fellowship with him while we are walking in darkness, we lie and do not do what is true" (1 John 1:6). Rensberger observed,

> Internal conflicts have torn this community whose tradition was pervaded by the claim to truth. Now truth must be separated from falsehood within the community, and it is this that 1 John sets out to do, by subjecting claims of relationship with God to the test of ethical consistency.[27]

John next draws an additional conclusion. God forgives the sins of

[27]David Rensberger, *1 John, 2 John, 3 John* (Nashville: Abingdon Press, 1997) 52

those who emulate his *koinonia*. There is no darkness in God. There should be no darkness in those who claim to be God's. Darkness in those who claim to be God's results from dropping out of the fellowship of believers.

> Fellowship with one another may be another way of speaking about love, so that imitating God in light and love brings fellowship both with God and with one another. Fellowship with God is thus not a private relationship but involves joining with others in shared tradition . . . and in love. We can walk in the light only when we walk with others whom we can love and with whom we can learn of God.[28]

God, who himself is *koinonia*, does not receive those who turn their back on *koinonia*. ". . . but if we walk in the light as he himself is in the light, we have fellowship with one another, and the blood of Jesus his Son cleanses us from all sin" (1 John 1:7).

The conclusion is stark. Those who have fellowship one with another are continually receiving the forgiveness of their sins because of the blood of Jesus Christ, the Son of God. Those who have departed from the fellowship, that is the church, are no longer in the light, but in darkness. Their sins are no longer being forgiven. 1 John has a "high" doctrine of the church in that the forgiveness of sins occurs only when one is involved in the fellowship—the *koinonia* of the church. According to 1 John, the church dispenses the forgiveness of sins. But forgiveness of sins occurs, not through specially ordained functionaries in the church, but because of the fellowship of the whole church as it engages in the mission of Christ.

These persons about whom John writes have a wrongheaded ecclesiology as a result of their bad theology. For them, just as it necessary for God to keep his distance from humans, it is also quite appropriate for humans to distance themselves from those of inferior or lackadaisical religious commitment. The crisis in the churches to whom John wrote came

[28] *Ibid.*, 52-53.

about as the result of certain "superior" Christians departing and therefore destroying *koinonia*. "They went out from us, but they did not belong to us; for if they had belonged to us, they would have remained with us. But by going out they made it plain that none of them belongs to us" (1 John 2:19). Bad theology results in bad ecclesiology. For John the church has a salvific function. The fellowship of the Christians in the church is the basis upon which sins are forgiven. "If we walk in the light as he himself is in the light, we have fellowship with one another, and the blood of Jesus his Son cleanses us from all sin" (1 John 1:7). Those who depart from fellowship are no longer receiving the grace of God distributed through the blood in his church.

In this opening section John has focused upon the fountainhead of fellowship—the God who is eager to fellowship human persons. He sent his Son so that he could be seen, heard, and touched. God does not hold humanity off at arm's length. He enters into the very life of human beings. Humans, in turn, are to be there for each other. God is not the deus absconditus, "the disappearing God." He is the God who breaks into the very lives of humans through the incarnation, that is, the enfleshing of his Son. We have the privilege of depicting the God of Scripture who wants to "reach out and touch" humankind made in his image. God is *koinonia* and *agape*!

chapter 4

SIN AND JESUS CHRIST, THE ATONING SACRIFICE 1 John 1:8-2:17

It is Christ who makes fellowship possible. God is holy and he requires holy believers. Believers are holy, however, not because of their superior esoteric experiences and spiritual exercises. They are holy only because the blood of Jesus Christ the Son cleanses them from all sin. "But if anyone does sin, we have an advocate with the Father, Jesus Christ the righteous; and he is the atoning sacrifice for our sins, and not for ours only but also for the sins of the whole world" (1 John 2:1-2). This forgiveness is not parceled out to each individual believer by the Son, however, but as the result of the *koinonia* of all the believers. "But if we walk in the light as he himself is in the light, we have fellowship with one another, and the blood of Jesus his Son cleanses us from all sin" (1 John 1:7). What a redemptive powerhouse the fellowship of the church is! Through this fellowship we appropriate the Christ-secured and freely offered forgiveness of sins.

After identifying the capability of the blood of Christ in forgiving sins, John turns to a rather lengthy set of observations on sin and forgiveness. First, he affirms beyond a shadow of a doubt that sin is pervasive. "If we say that we have no sin, we deceive ourselves, and the truth is not in us" (1 John 1:8). Why does he make this claim at this point? It could be that he does so to prevent some from saying that they do not need the fellowship of the church. They have not sinned to begin with.

But this seems unlikely. Probably those who departed made some claim about perfection. It is not clear exactly what their claim may have been. It is known that a century or more after the Epistle was written some Gnostics claimed perfection upon the ground that they were born of God who was perfect. Others claimed that being born of God redeemed their soul so that though their fleshy self might commit sin, the spiritual self that is what ultimately counts, does not.

Perkins thinks that most likely those who departed claimed perfection and may have even downplayed the significance of the death of Christ as the atonement for sins.

> The evidence of our gnostic writings, however, suggests that the problem might have been a claim to perfection based on moral and ascetic seriousness; a seriousness which led to denial of a divine forgiveness mediated by baptism or the sacrificial death of Jesus. Such writings insist that each person must achieve perfection through his or her knowledge and ascetic practice. One must conquer the passions of the soul and become free from attachment to the material world or body. Several late 2nd century or 3rd century texts explicitly attack the orthodox claim that the death of Jesus atones for sin. A tract which preaches severe asceticism as the way to salvation, *Testimony of Truth*, says that any God who would demand a human sacrifice would be vain-glorious, and could not be the true God . . . Such a claim did not imply moral laxity or the claim that gnostics cannot sin no matter what they do.[29]

John wants to make sure that it is perfectly clear, however, despite the pervasiveness of sin in even the believer's life, that sin will be forgiven upon confession. This confession may be privately addressed to God. But if one's sins have been exposed publicly, then it is appropriate to make confession before the body of Christ, that is, the church. "If we confess

[29]Pheme Perkins, *The Johannine Epistles*, 19.

our sins, he who is faithful and just will forgive us our sins and cleanse us from all unrighteousness" (1 John 1:9). Horatio G. Spafford declared this resplendent forgiveness in the second verse of the favorite century-old hymn, "It Is Well with My Soul."

> *My sin—Oh, the bliss of this glorious tho't*
> *—My sin, not in part but the whole,*
> *Is nailed to the cross and I bear it no more:*
> *Praise the Lord, praise the Lord, O my soul!*

John once again repeats the declaration that those who claim they have not sinned make Jesus a liar. In seems unnecessary for him to repeat this charge unless someone in the Johannine communities actually maintained sinlessness. Most likely this was the claim of those who departed.

John continues his comments on sin into Chapter 2. He addresses his readers as little children, or simply children, 19 times in 1, 2, and 3 John, and once in the Gospel. Early commentators, assuming that John lived into the 90's A. D., took this designation to be the result of John's elderly status. It also certainly is a term of endearment regardless of the age of the author. John affirms that he will do everything in his power to encourage the believers on to perfection. "I am writing these things to you so that you may not sin" (1 John 2:1). But again John underlined the fact that if sin does occur, it was Jesus who through his death provided the sacrifice for their sin. A focus upon Jesus giving his life as a sacrifice for sin is not emphasized in the Johannine writings, but in the Gospel, John the Baptist identified him as "the Lamb of God who takes away the sin of the world!" (John 1:29). Because Jesus made an atoning sacrifice for sin, the believer has an advocate with the Father.

> The baptized christian should not sin, but if he does, the author assures him that Jesus stands as his heavenly advocate. This approach is quite different from the elaborate rules about loss of food, table fellowship, community rank, and temporary or permanent exclusion from the community which the Essenes used to

deal with the sins of those who had entered its new covenant.[30]

The word translated "Advocate" is the Greek word *paraklētos*, which occurs several times in the Gospel of John and refers to the Holy Spirit (John 14:26). In this case it is the Son himself who is the advocate for the believer who has committed a sin. The believer is called to live as sinless a life as possible, as is obvious from the charge not to love the world (1 John 2:15-17). We will make detailed comment on this passage later. But if the believers do sin, and they are in fellowship with those who are Christ's, then their sins will be forgiven and in that sense they are sinless. They are sinless, not because of their skills at avoiding sins on their own, perhaps a position of the secessionists, but they are sinless because the blood of Christ continually makes possible the forgiveness of their sins.

In respect to Jesus Christ designated "the righteous," Schnackenburg wrote,

> Jesus Christ is also distinguished with the epithet, "righteous" . . . God will not abandon the advocacy of those who "do righteousness," who conform to his will (cf. I John 3:7) . . . It is still more probable that the author adds this to show how Jesus became our Advocate before the throne of God. It is because he died "as the righteous for thc unrightcous" . . . or because he offered himself for sinners as a holy and blameless high priest (cf. Heb. 7:26f).[31]

In 1 John 2:2, John affirms that Christ atoned for the sins, not only of those in the community of faith, but for the sins of the whole world. What can he mean by this? Does he mean that not only those in the faith community receive forgiveness of their sins through Christ, but also those of all humans who have ever been and will be alive in the future? This seems doubtful, since he thinks that the believers whose sins are being forgiven are in fellowship with the Johannine bodies of believers. He also thinks

[30]*Ibid.*, 20.
[31]Rudolf Schnackenburg, *The Johannine Epistles*, 87.

that the sins of those who departed are not being forgiven. They are the antichrists! (1 John 3:18). His point seems to be the same as John 3:16, "For God so loved the world that he gave his only Son, so that everyone who believes in him may not perish but may have eternal life." The "world" most of the time in the Gospel is not so much the material earth but people who live their life apart from God and are alienated from him.[32] God gave his Son for the world; Christ even died for the world! This eternal life is available to all in the world. But in order to receive it, they must believe that "Jesus is the Messiah, the Son of the living God" (John 20:31). So here also in 1 John, Jesus Christ the righteous is the atoning sacrifice for the sins of the whole world (2:1-2). But in order to receive this forgiveness it is imperative to confess Jesus. "God abides in those who confess that Jesus is the Son of God, and they abide in God. So we have known and believe the love that God has for us" (1 John 4:15-16).

Rensberger suggests that John employs the phrase "for the sins of the whole world" (1 John 2:2) so as to underline the prospect for the addition of others to the communities of faith who do not at the time of his writing believe.

> That Jesus is the atonement not just for the sins of the Johannine Christian community but for those of the whole world is a remarkably inclusive statement for the otherwise often closed and world-rejecting 1 John . . . It is probably derived from John 1:29, and implies that for the author the possibility of mission to the world is still open, that opportunity remains to bring the "word of life" to those totally outside the Christian community. The double Johannine attitude toward the world, as an object of salvation and as hostile to both Savior and saved, appears in 1 John in the sharpest possible contrast.[33]

Schnackenburg thinks that the emphasis on Christ dying for the sins of

[32]Thomas H. Olbricht, "Its Works are Evil (John 7:7)," *Restoration Quarterly*, 7:4 (1963) 242-244.
[33]Rensberger, *1 John*, 57.

the whole world also contrasts with the views of those who left. "This is hardly comparable to the arrogance of the gnostics, who as pneumatics think that they are superior to the suffering incurred as a punishment for sin."[34] John now for the first time introduces the word "know" (givōskō in Greek).

> Now by this we may be sure that we know him, if we obey his commandments. Whoever says, "I have come to know him," but does not obey his commandments, is a liar, and in such a person the truth does not exist; but whoever obeys his word, truly in this person the love of God has reached perfection (1 John 2:3-5).

We have derived the English word "gnostic" from this basic root givsk. "Know," translating givsk, occurs 22 times in 1 John. Another Greek word (oida) translated "know" occurs 15 times in the Epistle. Because of the constant employment of "know," it is almost certain that the separatists set forth claims about knowing God or Christ in some sort of a unique manner. John has a basically simple test for determining whether or not a specific person knows God. The one who knows God obeys his commands. Knowing God is therefore not a rigorous intellectual pursuit or some highly volatile illumination. To know him is to enter into a trusting relationship with God that results in a joyful keeping of his commands.

On good grounds Schnackenburg concludes,

> The author of 1 John takes over the phrase "knowledge of God" from the heretical teachers he is opposing. It is significant he uses the term, alongside of "seeing God" for a direct vision of God (1 John 3:6; cf. John 14:7, 17; 3 John 11) . . . They are convinced that they are "in the light" (2:9). Their goal is their own divination; "this is the glorious goal for all, to have acquired gnosis: to become divinized." Or again, those who have acquired gnosis are

[34]Schackensburg, *The Johannine Epistles*, 88.

good and holy; indeed they are already divine. It is possible that the gnostics of 1 John were not so precise about the way such knowledge of God was achieved, though they may have encouraged ecstatic visions of God (4:12, 20; 3:6b) . . . It is not ecstasy that lies at the heart of gnosticism but deliverance from the world of darkness, of the material, and of death, and the return of the soul into the realm of light from which it had come and to which it yearns to return from this alien world . . . At the same time contempt for all material reality, which is characteristic of this type of spirituality, provides a strong impulse toward ecstasy.[35]

It is clear that John had a different understanding of what is involved in knowing God. On this Schnackenburg wrote:

> The Christian, on the other hand, believes in a revelation that happened at a particular moment in history and became the subject of public proclamation (1 John 1:3, 5). The Christian receives this revelation at the hands of messengers. It is not imparted in a secret rite of initiation nor through some exalted dream, but by listening faithfully to the divine message (1 John 2:7, 24; 3:11).[36]

At different times in the history of Christendom people have developed an interest in a unique knowledge of God that is ecstatic and private. For many a saving knowledge of God is dependent upon an ecstatic experience. John Wesley at Aldersgate Street (May 24, 1738) "felt his heart strangely warmed." For John in this letter the knowing of God consists of hearing what was revealed that could be heard, seen, and touched, a public manifestation of God (1 John 1:1-3). In the twenty-first century many seek an ecstatic experience of God that leads to assurance, certainly an exuberance regarding God's presence. This may, in fact, be received

[35]*Ibid.*, 92-93.
[36]*Ibid.*, 93-94.

in the presence of others, but is known within. Exterior manifestations may occur such as speaking in tongues, laughing, or dancing. For John rather, the experience of or anointment by God leads to a desire to keep the commandments of God. The singular commandment John focused upon was the loving of other believers. "Whoever loves a brother or sister lives in the light, and in such a person there is no cause for stumbling" (1 John 2:10). "We know love by this, that he laid down his life for us—and we ought to lay down our lives for one another" (1 John 3:16).

Schnackenburg has put it well,

> But the question of moral behavior becomes for the Christians the overriding concern, when seen in the light of their Savior's ethical requirements. Whoever would know God and attain to fellowship with him must keep his commandments (2:3-5). God's emissary is not a prototype of the Christian destiny, individual and cosmic, but a pattern for moral behavior in this world (2:6). More than this, the Son of God made man makes highly concrete demands on the Christian, for the Son is the source of redemption; and for that the Christian owes a debt of gratitude (2:1f). Primarily this means the love of brother and sister (2:7ff). Moral obedience is the indispensable condition for eternal salvation, which even though expected joyfully and with confidence (2:28; 4:17) continues to be more than a matter of hope (3:3).[37]

John is explicit on the demand to love fellow believers.

> Whoever says, "I have come to know him," but does not obey his commandments, is a liar, and in such a person the truth does not exist; but whoever obeys his word, truly in this person the love of God has reached perfection (1 John 2:4-5).

The one who knows God abides in him. The one who knows Christ

[37] *Ibid.*, 95.

"ought to walk just as he walked" (1 John 2:6). J. W. Roberts appropriately observed,

> John is not concerned with acts of worship in religious services in his discussions in these books. He is primarily concerned with ethical relations with one's neighbor or brother and the injunctions of Jesus to walk in the light, that is, in purity of life (3:3). The proof is in the doing. The reality of Jesus and what he can mean to one's soul is realized in walking as he walked (vs. 6), in "walking in the light as he is in the light." [38]

John now takes up the commandment that the churches had from the beginning. His comments at this point make it clear that "from the beginning," has to do with what transpired during the earthly reign of Jesus. The old commandment, which was new when given, is the love commandment.

> I give you a new commandment, that you love one another. Just as I have loved you, you also should love one another. By this everyone will know that you are my disciples, if you have love for one another (John 13:34-35).

John makes essentially the same point in 2 John 5-6.

> But now, dear lady, I ask you, not as though I were writing you a new commandment, but one we have had from the beginning, let us love one another. And this is love, that we walk according to his commandments; this is the commandment just as you have heard it from the beginning—you must walk in it.

We should also consider that one of the fundamental teachings to new believers in the Johannine churches had to do with loving one

[38]J. W. Roberts, *The Letters of John* (Austin: R. B. Sweet Co., Inc, 1968) 41.

another. "The beginning," therefore, in this case was the key message of love given upon entry into the community. There is a story from the early church which underlines the importance of the teaching on love. As John grew older, so the story goes he had to be carried to the place of assembly on a pallet. Most of the time he just lay there absorbing the teaching and singing. At the end of the assembly, out of deference to his status as an original disciple and his long years of service, he was asked if he had anything to say. Each time he sat up on his pallet and stated in his weak voice, "Love one another!" Central to walking in the commandments of Christ is to love one another.

In 2:9-11 John returns to the metaphor of light and darkness, apparently a favorite metaphor of those who left. For them it had to do with their enlightenment from God, probably achieved in an ecstatic experience. They further belittled the believers who had not had such an experience by describing their circumstances as still being in darkness. John moves light and darkness from the realm of ecstasy into the world of concrete existence. To be in the light is to love one's fellow believers. To be in the darkness is to hate, that is, to turn one's back on them. So, according to John, those who left, in fact, demonstrated by that act that they had not received the real light from God which transformed the self so they could love the fellow believers, not walking out on them. "Whoever loves a brother or sister lives in the light" (1 John 2:10). "But whoever hates another believer is in darkness" (1 John 2:11).

The next section, 2:12-14, is an effort to assure those who remained behind that they stood in good stead with God, had been properly taught, and were appropriately grounded in the genuine faith. This section seems to exhibit the form of regularized instruction. It is noteworthy that in all likelihood all these declarations relate to the claims of those who left. The affirmations are directed toward children, young people, and fathers. The children are assured that their sins are forgiven because of his name, that is the name of the Lord Jesus Christ. Those who departed apparently claimed purity based upon their recently anointed status rather than because of the blood of Jesus Christ. The fathers are affirmed because they know him who is from the beginning, that is Jesus Christ. They do not, therefore, need a new enlightenment in order to enter God's orbit. The young people are worthy because they have conquered the evil one. Those who departed, because of their experiential rapprochement with deity, likely claimed immunity from any powers of evil.

John now enters into a second set of assurances, taking up the three in order again. The children are on solid ground because they know the Father. They do not need to take a back seat to those secessionists who claimed that knowing the Father involved an esoteric anointment. The fathers need no latter day rain or illumination because they "know him who is from the beginning" (1 John 2:14), a point repeated. The young people are commendable because they are strong. They aren't, as those who left likely asserted, anemic believers simply because they have not tasted the new fad regarding ecstatic experience. Furthermore, the faithful are not without directives. The secessionists likely claimed the privilege of special Deity leading. They have the correct direction because the "word of God abides in you" (1 John 2:14). As stated before, in addition, they have "overcome the evil one."

Following these efforts at encouragement to the different age groups, John insists that the root of sin is the love of the world. The love of the world needs to be redirected so as to love the Savior and the saved. "Do not love the world or the things in the world" (1 John 2:15). The specific forms of love for the world are "the desire of the flesh, the desire of the eyes [and] the pride in riches" (1 John 2:16). The problem with the world is that it is contingent, that is, subject to decay and destruction. The world is finite, whereas God is infinite. "Those who do the will of God live forever" (1 John 2:17). It is a genuine question, therefore, as to why the desires of the world are so alluring to those who know the love of God. Should believers turn away from the world, they will reject its desires and live the life God demands.

Regarding this section Amos Wilder appropriately wrote,

> But in our present passage world means more than "mankind fallen away from God."...For him there is a great contrast between God and the creation. Eternal life and the true light

> and the Spirit belong to the original order ("in the beginning") from which "the Son of God has come and has given us understanding" (5:20). The world is created and loved by God, and Christ has come to save it. But it is ephemeral, subject to decay and death; moreover, it has fallen under the control of the evil one, and therefore into darkness. The world of men and the world of nature were closely interrelated in the thought of ancient men. Thus in our present passage not only the lusts of a fallen humanity but a love of the creature and the creation is disparaged over against the primal and everlasting ground of existence, the Father and his purpose.[39]

Some of the older commentators suggested that the sources for all possible sins may be subsumed under the three categories set out by John. Furthermore, the claim has been made that the three duplicate the three temptations of Jesus. The first category of sin, the desire of the flesh, corresponds to Satan's charge to Jesus that, because he had fasted for forty days, he should change a stone into bread. Jesus resisted that temptation by declaring that "man does not live by bread alone" (Matthew 3:4). The second category is desire of the eyes. Perhaps this is a bit of a stretch when compared with the second temptation of Jesus, yet the second temptation has to do with observed actions of Jesus in which he is challenged to exhibit his immunity to the harm that would befall an ordinary mortal. "If you are the Son of God, throw yourself down." If you are preserved in the fall despite your recklessness, Satan implies, we will be able to see that you have the characteristics of Deity. Jesus replied, "Do not put the Lord your God to the test" (Matthew 4:7). The third sin category is the pride in riches. Satan took Jesus to the top of a very high mountain and showed him the kingdoms of the world and said to him, "All these I will give you, if you will fall down and worship me" (Matthew 4:9). Jesus resisted this pride in ownership by replying, "Worship the Lord your God, and serve

[39]Amos N. Wilder, "The First, Second, and Third Epistles of John," *The Interpreter's Bible* (Nashville: Abingdon Press, 1957) 238.

only him" (Matthew 4:10). In each case Jesus responded to the tempter by quoting Scripture. The Hebrews writer declared that Jesus was tempted in all points like as we, yet was without sin (Hebrews 4:15). Jesus, so Hebrews declared, faced all the categories of sin and therefore was confronted by the same temptations that challenge all humans.

John will return to sin and its consequences in Chapter 3 of the Epistle. In the section we have just completed it is obvious that the believer is challenged to overcome sin. John sees sin as the failure to love those who have accepted Jesus Christ as the focus of their life. Sin festers from hatred. But should one sin, Jesus Christ the righteous has already given his life for the atonement of those who trust him. They must exhibit the love for the Lord in concrete fellowship. "But if we walk in the light as he himself is in the light, we have fellowship with one another, and the blood of Jesus his Son cleanses us from all sin" (1 John 1:7).

chapter 5

THEY WENT OUR FROM US, BUT THEY DID NOT BELONG TO US 1 John 2:18-29

John has provided hints regarding the views of the separatists through underlining God's fellowship through Christ, human fellowship of one with another, as well as claims about knowledge and sinlessness. Now John no longer camouflages the breach. He makes it explicit that some "went out from us" (1 John 2:19). Why did these people leave, and what does John see as the context for their leaving?

John addresses his readers once again as children. This time the term is not for a group within the believers. He addresses all those who remain as his children. We now learn for the first time that John perceives the departure as a sign that it is the last hour. Regarding the last hour, Kysar wrote,

> Last hour means the final period before the concluding act of God in the history of the world and humanity. It is used in this document only here and in v. 18. The more common NT designation is "last day(s)" . . . The use of hour rather than "day(s)" is a peculiar variation which may be an intentional effort to declare the nearness of the decisive time. It may also be that the Johannine tradition in which Jesus' glorification in the cross is spoken of as "hour" (e. g., John 2:4; 7:30; 8:20) has influenced

our author.[40]

John now declares that they have been apprised of the coming of the antichrist and that the numbers of departed are several. This critical development therefore pinpoints the departure as the last hour (1 John 2:18). Rendsberger concludes that,

> The notion of antichrist, that is, an "anti-Messiah," is not found at all in - Jewish literature, nor in Christian literature except where it is dependent on 1 and 2 John (e.g. Polycarp, *Phil.* 7:1). The closest precedent is the idea of the "pseudochrist" or false messiah in Mark 13. Thus, "antichrist is coming" may originally have been a warning against a false messiah.[41]

The term "Antichrist" has become the favorite appellation of those who anticipate the arising of an apocalyptic evil one or force against Christ and the Christian faith in the end-time. Any evil being mentioned in the Scripture is called the Antichrist by these modern interpreters, for example, in Revelation the "beast" of 11:7, the "red dragon" of Chapter 12, the beast "having seven heads and ten horns" of 13 and 17, or perhaps even Satan himself. The "lawless one" of 2 Thessalonians 2:3 is likewise so identified. If one were to employ Bible names for Bible things, this widespread use of the term is unwarranted. In the Johannine Epistles the antichrist has a very specific referent. The antichrist is the one who denies that Jesus is the Christ (1 John 2:22). Furthermore, Rendsberger thinks that "the opponents were not merely fellow Johannine Christians who left the group, but teachers, people who were in a position to lead, or mislead others (vs. 27)."[42]

John makes clear in 2:19 that the people who had left were a part of the Johannine churches, "But by going out they made it plain that none

[40]Kysar, *I, II, III John*, 59.
[41]Rendsberger, *1 John, 2 John, 3 John*, 78.
[42]*Ibid.*

of them belonged to us" (1 John 2:19). So as to reassure those who remained, John reminded them that "you have been anointed by the Holy One, and all of you have knowledge" (1 John 2:20). From this it seems apparent that those who left made some claim to special anointment through the reception of esoteric knowledge. John has already guaranteed them that through what they had been taught from the beginning and through their reception of the Holy Spirit they possessed the truth. With these observations he is now ready to identify the false position those who left held. "Who is the liar but the one who denies that Jesus is the Christ?" (1 John 2:22). Furthermore, "This is the antichrist, the one who denies the Father and the Son" (1 John 2:22). The one who has the Father must of necessity believe that Jesus is the Son of God (1 John 2:23). John elaborates on their position in 1 John 4:2 "By this you know the Spirit of God; every spirit that confesses that Jesus Christ has come in the flesh is from God, and every spirit that does not confess Jesus is not from God." Those who left confessed that Christ the Son came upon Jesus, but that Jesus was a human and not from God.

Strecker thinks that the best description of those who left is Docetism, which he distinguishes from Gnosticism. He thinks that their views are something like those of Cerinthus, but that not enough is known about his views to be sure. On the secessionists' Docetic Christology he wrote,

> It is applied to the earthly life of Jesus of Nazareth, his birth, his suffering, and his death. Since all this cannot be reconciled with the idea of a divinity that, as such, is impassible and removed from the coming to be and passing away of worldly things, the Christian confession of the saving significance of the person of Jesus Christ can only be understood in such a way that a sharp distinction is drawn between Christ, the Son of God (the heavenly human one, the Christ above, etc.) and the earthly human being Jesus of Nazareth. Only the latter suffered and died on the cross, while the former was united with Jesus only temporarily "in appearance." Consequently, Docetism opposes the doctrine

> of the incarnation, for it is a fundamental truth that the divine cannot unite with the human, the heavenly with the earthly. This christological conception, nourished by the Greek spirit, could be articulated in a variety of systems.[43]

In view of the current climate, it is appropriate to comment on the ease with which Christians depart from one congregation or from one denomination or fellowship to another. The reason often given is that the church from which they departed no longer fills their needs. They are no longer being fed. Explanations normally involve criticisms of various sorts regarding the inferiority of the people and theology of their former associates. Those of this mindset are of the predisposition that the benefit of the doubt always belongs to the one who departs, not to the one who stays. They seem to think, in overthrowing their current connection, they have the long history of God's relationship with his people on their side.

This current consensus on leaving a church has little support from the Scripture generally or from John. John seems to think that it is those who stay who please God. They are the ones who are Christ-like, unless Christ is a Docetic Christ. Christ came from the Father into the human material world, a realm far inferior to the one from which he descended. He came to redeem and lift up the fallen. John thinks that believers who find themselves among the less commendable Christians need to stay around so as to encourage and assist in spiritual growth. Who can better lead others into the right path?

Recently I read several essays written by those who had left the Christian heritage in which they were nurtured. What struck me about the "those who left" essays is that all assert that it is God's will that they left. Most do not entertain the prospect that it might be God's will for anyone to stay. There are good grounds in the Scripture for staying. None of the prophets of Israel were called by God to leave Israel behind, even though they were sometimes called to speak to other peoples. God called them to speak a word of condemnation, repentance, confession, and for-

[43]Georg Strecker, *The Johannine Letters* (Minneapolis: Fortress Press, 1996) 71.

Francis Burl Curtis ('50), 90, of Searcy died June 6, 2020. He received a master's from Harding School of Theology in 1975. For 17 years, he and his wife worked in the mission field in South Carolina where he preached for five congregations, planting three of the five. Side by side, they conducted home Bible studies, campaigns, Bible camps, Vacation Bible Schools, and owned and operated a Christian book store. They conducted more than 100 Bible teacher workshops in 12 states. They also operated Curtis Kindergarten in Searcy, caring for preschool and kindergarten students for more than 30 years. During his lifetime, he wrote hundreds of articles published primarily in *Carolina Christian* magazine and *Gospel Light*. He was passionate about his work with Truth for Today World Mission School, where he served on the board of directors. He is survived by his wife of 70 years, **Mary Evelyn Hayes** ('53); four children, **Larry** ('77), **Rebecca McLain** ('79), Beth Hoofman and **Kevin** ('94); 14 grandchildren; and seven great-grandchildren.

…of Christ some left behind the typical …laves by the Dead Sea designated the …t hear any mention of these communi… …ist, Jesus did not single them out for spe…

…all departed Galilee for Jerusalem. They …selves Israel—the new Israel. In Jerusalem …continued their Jewish practices regarding …e temple. "One day Peter and John were …hour of prayer, at three o'clock in the after… …e saw Peter and John about to go into the temple, … alms" (Acts 3:3). "But during the night an angel of the Lord opened the prison doors, brought them out, and said, 'Go stand in the temple and tell the people the whole message about this life.' When they heard this, they entered the temple at daybreak and went on with their teaching" (Acts 5:19-21). These early Christians did not abandon the ways of their ancestors. They remained faithful and taught the new way of God to salvation—through Jesus the Son who died on the cross at Golgotha.

Paul did not perceive that God called him to leave Judaism. He affirmed in Romans that God called him to bring Judaism to a faith in the Messiah, and especially to be an apostle to the Gentiles. In Romans 9-11 Paul argued that his conversion of Gentiles was contributing to the bringing of his ethnic people—the Jews—to a belief in Jesus as Messiah. Paul always considered himself to be a Jew—a Messianic Jew. It is only second-century Christians who saw themselves as standing over against Judaism.

So at minimum I conclude that God is more interested in his people staying and bringing people into an enhanced relationship with him than he is in them leaving. So leaving may be an option—perhaps in some cases a necessary option. But it may not be that for which God has called most of us. He may be calling most of us to bring those of our religious heritage to a new appreciation and legitimate perception of him. I say this regarding whatever heritage it is in which one finds oneself. If you have new insight regarding God from his word, stay it out and share it with those with whom you are associated. The time may come, though, when present associates can no longer tolerate these new insights into the ways of God. Paul sometimes was barred from synagogues. But he didn't turn his back on the synagogue because he considered these former associates inferior. He left when they evicted him.

> When Silas and Timothy arrived from Macedonia, Paul was occupied with proclaiming the word, testifying to the Jews that the Messiah was Jesus. When they opposed and reviled him, in protest he shook the dust from his clothes and said to them, "Your blood be on your own heads? I am innocent. From now on I will go to the Gentiles." Then he left the synagogue and went to the house of Titius Justus, a worshiper of God; his house was next door to the synagogue (Acts 18:5-7).

In the remaining section of chapter 2, John challenges the readers to abide and retain confidence in their status before God. Because of the nature of his remarks it seems that those who left denigrated the status and commitment of their fellow believers. The secessionists had moved ahead to new enlightenment, to an anointing which positioned them in a much more favorable relationship with God as well as a superior confidence. The rhetoric of those departing left those who stayed behind bewildered and confused. They were on the verge, as we would say in the twenty-first century, of developing an inferiority complex. Kysar has astutely observed,

> The author thus gives the readers reason to trust their present stand and reject the effort of the separatists to sway them. They have in their initial beginnings in the gospel and in the gift of the Spirit the true understanding of the faith, and they are exhorted to remain faithful to that view. They are protected from the falsehood of the separatists by their experiences in the community. It is important that the author ask the readers in a time of uncertainty, when their confidence is challenged, to return to

> their "roots" in faith—their "beginning" and their "anointing." As Israel gained its confidence in times of trial by remembering its past history, the church is urged to tap the source of its stability—what God has done for it in the past.[44]

John first summons his readers to abide in what they learned at the beginning. It was good solid teaching. It will place them in good stead with the Son and the Father (1 John 2:21). The outcome of the believers abiding will be "eternal life." The separatists may have moved to an overly realized eschatology in which they claimed that they had already entered into life eternal. Specific persons with these views are denounced in 2 Timothy 2:17-18, "Hymenaeus and Philetus, who have swerved from the truth by claiming that the resurrection has already taken place." John makes clear that this life, though, perhaps already being enjoyed or inaugurated; nevertheless, the future is to be fully realized "at his coming" (1 John 2:28).

He also reminds them that they were anointed at the beginning with the Holy Spirit or *paraklētos*. "But you have been anointed by the Holy One, and all of you have knowledge" (1 John 2:20). Whatever the enlightenment or anointment those who departed boasted of, John assures those who remain that they were anointed at the beginning of their Christian journey. And this anointment also is a part of the teaching from the first. These statements about the anointing here are reminiscent of declarations made by Jesus in the Gospel. The coming of the *paraklētos* will be involved in providing believers with the appropriate instructions (John 14:26). "But the Advocate, the Holy Spirit, whom the Father will send in my name, will teach you everything, and remind you of all that I have said to you." Also, "When the Spirit of truth comes, he will guide you into all the truth; for he will not speak on his own, but will speak whatever he hears, and will declare to you the things that are to come" (John 16:12-13). We know from the Epistle that this promise in the Gospel is not for just the twelve, since John tells the believers to

[44]Kysar, *I, II, III John*, 66-67.

which he writes of essentially the same work of the Spirit in them that they will enjoy. "As for you, the anointing that you received from him abides in you, and so you do not need anyone to teach you" (1 John 2:27). The believers who remain have been anointed in the true manner, and they need to abide in these teachings rather than take up the esoteric later experiences of those who departed.

The body of believers—the church—is cleansed through *koinonia*. It is a *koinonia* made possible by the very death of the Son of God—maker of heaven and earth. Those in the fellowship of John's churches weren't somehow missing out on the anointed insight—a special *gnosis* or knowledge claimed by those who left. Those who remained had that knowledge and were in no way inferior. They possessed that knowledge from the beginning. "I write to you, fathers, because you know him who is from the beginning" (1 John 2:14). That knowledge is bestowed upon the believer by the Holy Spirit at the beginning when one affirms that "Jesus Christ has come in the flesh" (1 John 4:2). Believers who truly heard the Gospel when they first believed do not require another "baptism," that of the Spirit, or a second blessing, in order to please God and bask in the *koinonia* of God's people.

John ends this section by charging the believers to abide in Christ. If they so abide, they will be confident and not put to shame at the coming of Jesus Christ (1 John 2:28). If they know Christ as righteous, they will realize that they are going to be with God. Christ was righteous because he did what was right according to the will of God. "I have come down from heaven, not to do my own will, but the will of him who sent me" (John 6:38). They likewise may be bold before God when they do his will. "You may be sure that everyone who does right has been born of him" (1 John 2:29). Being born of God does not come with some esoteric Gnostic-type experience. It is what the believers experienced from the beginning by being born of the water and the Spirit. "I tell you, no one can enter the kingdom of God without being born of water and Spirit" (John 3:5). They can furthermore ascertain whether or not that was truly a birth from above by what they do. If they do what is right, they are born of him.

chapter 6

ALL WHO HAVE THIS HOPE IN HIM PURIFY THEMSELVES 1 John 3:1-24

Believers are to be holy because God is holy (Leviticus 19:2). Believers in Christ have a new and incredible incentive to be Christ-like. It resides in the Father's inexplicable gift of love. "See what love the Father has given us, that we should be called the children of God" (1 John 3:1). Believers are not holy because of what they have done, but because of what God has done through the death of his Son. "We love because he first loved us" (1 John 4:19). Because of the Father's great love, even sinful humans may be called "the children of God."

> But to all who received him, who believed in his name, he gave power to become children of God, who were born, not of blood or of the will of the flesh or of the will of man, but of God (John 1:12-13).

As long as believers persevere in *koinonia*, they will continue in forgiveness (1 John 1:7). In the end-time believers will be like their Lord (1 John 3:2)! They must now open themselves to the work of God so as to attain their purity. "And all who have this hope in him purify themselves, just as he is pure" (1 John 3:3). "Those who have been born of God do not sin, because God's seed abides in them; they cannot sin, because they have been born of God" (1 John 3:9). The Greek for "do not sin" is the middle verbal construction, that is, "they do not continue to sin." The presence of God overpowers the dominance of sin in the life of the believer. "But if anyone does sin, we have an advocate with the Father, Jesus Christ the righteous; and he is the atoning sacrifice for our sins" (1 John 2:1-2).

John affirms that although Christians know themselves as children of God, the community of unbelief either does not know or cannot fathom what that means. "The reason the world does not know us is that it did not know him" (1 John 3:1). Once again John makes a parallel statement in the first chapter of the Gospel, "He was in the world, and the world came into being through him; yet the world did not know him. He came to what was his own, and his own people did not accept him" (John 1:10-11). Believers do not yet know what they will be at the coming or revealing of the Lord. But of this they can be sure, "We will be like him, for we will see him as he is" (1 John 3:3). Should there be some claim of already being what God has in mind for his children, John assures his readers that the future has not already arrived. The separatists may have claimed otherwise. Though the exact nature of that future is unknown, it has not happened as yet and, when it does, the believer will be identical with Christ.

John now introduces the appropriate response to the fact that God has extended through his Son this magnificent gift of grace. The future hope for the believer is that he will, at that future time when Christ returns, be changed to be like him. "And all who have this hope in him purify themselves, just as he is pure" (1 John 3:3). Kysar wrote,

> Purifies himself, then, means to rid oneself of all those actions and attitudes which are inappropriate to one who lives in a saving relationship with Christ. It is the human's responsibility to prepare oneself for the eschatological day when Christians are made to be "as he is" and when they are immersed in the divine presence. The purity attributed to Christ, it follows, is a moral purity, and here the author implies the sinless perfection of Christ (a position made explicit in v. 5a below) which is found

elsewhere in the NT literature of the last quarter of the first century (e. g., Heb. 4:15).[45]

To be pure is to be sinless, and John now launches into a discussion of sin. He defines sin as lawlessness. Lawlessness is the attitude that there are no rules or laws defining the guidelines for life. Those who left may have held that, because of their special anointment, they lived above mundane sets of rules. J. W. Roberts wrote,

> John is concerned to point out the seriousness of misconduct. The Greek idea of sin is "missing the mark." It is a fault or failure to live at as high a standard as one might. This concept must not be construed as mere shortcoming, a failing to reach our potential. Sin in the Bible is much more serious. It is lawlessness or rebellion against God's revealed law. John is perhaps correcting the false teachers who tended to set themselves above sin (1:6, 8; 2:4) and who made acceptance with God a matter of mere knowledge or the performance of religious rites and the acceptance of revealed truth about religion. It must be remembered that there is a constant temptation in any system of religion to separate ethical and moral conduct from the practice of forms or rites of worship.[46]

Christ came, John declared, to take away sins, and he is sinless. He was pure, and to be like him is to emulate his purity. "No one who sins has either seen him or known him" (1 John 3:6). Believers should be wary of anyone who claims that purity of the soul is all that matters, not purity of life. Apparently certain teachers among those who left declared this, for John warns, "Let no one deceive you. Everyone who does what is right is righteous. Everyone who commits sin is a child of the devil" (1 John 3:7-8). The devil sinned from the beginning, so that those who sin are his

[45]*Ibid.*, 76.
[46]J. W. Roberts, *The Letters of John*, 79-80.

children, not children of God. The very reason that Jesus came was to destroy the works of the devil. If overt sin is of no consequence, then Christ's purpose in becoming human is without justification.

At this point John makes a statement that has amazed and puzzled biblical interpreters through the centuries. "Those who have been born of God do not sin, because God's seed abides in them; they cannot sin, because they have been born of God" (1 John 3:9). He had before this declared, "No one who abides in him sins" (1 John 3:5). What can John possibly mean? This seems a contradiction of his previous assertion, "But if anyone does sin, we have an advocate with the Father, Jesus Christ the righteous; and he is the atoning sacrifice for our sins" (1 John 2:1-2). The commentators have taken various positions on this matter. Raymond Brown has collected several of them and should be consulted if there is an interest in multiple positions.[47] Here I will present a few recommended interpretations.

One possibility is that John is speaking paradoxically. Just as in his view there are two sorts of people in the world, those who believe that Jesus is the Messiah and those who do not, he also is interested in distinguishing ideally the person whose life is Christ-like from those whose lives are not. In each case, therefore, he sets forth the extreme and thereby overstates the case. The ideal disciple is one who does not sin. Since his birth is from above or from God and he is a child of God, it follows to reason that in the absolute sense he cannot sin. But John concludes that this ideal is seldom realized, for he writes, "If we say we have no sin, we deceive ourselves and the truth is not in us" (1 John 1:8). According to J. W. Roberts, contrasting 1:8 with 3:9,

> In the first passage John combats the perfectionist who claims that he has risen above sin; in the present passage [3:9] he combats the immoralist (who might even be the same person) who claims that sin does not matter as long as one is born of God. The point is that sinlessness is the absolute standard and the only

[47]Raymond Brown, *The Epistles of John* (Garden City, NY: Doubleday, 1982) 402-435. See also his bibliography.

one consistent with the nature of sonship.[48]

Another proposal is that the Greek verbs indicate a continuing action. The Greek for "do not sin" is the middle verbal construction implying continuing action, that is, "they do not continue to sin." Sin, therefore, is not an overriding force in the life of the believer. One is not, as Paul puts it, "a slave to sin" (Romans 6:17). The presence of God overpowers the dominance of sin in the life of the believer. One may therefore sin, but the believer succeeds with the aid of the Holy Spirit in overcoming any persistent sin. Furthermore, those who continue in the fellowship of believers constantly have their sins remitted. "If we walk in the light as he himself is in the light, we have fellowship with one another and, and the blood of Jesus his Son cleanses us from all sin" (1 John 1:7). It seems to me that this second explanation is the more likely of the two.

Kysar makes a third proposal. He argues that sin in the gospel ". . .is understood primarily in terms of unbelief" (John 15:22-24; 16:9).[49] From this point of view, "The Christian cannot, then, sin in the sense of disbelief, for by definition one who 'abides in him' and 'has seen' and 'known him' is one who believes."[50] While this proposal has merit, I still think the second explanation is the better one. While leaving the fellowship of believers may be subsumed under disbelief, it seems to be that abdicating is the principle sin under consideration in the Johannine letters. But perhaps even more important is the false theology that justified the departure.

Kysar summarizes this section,

> In vv. 4-10 the author has again hammered at the point that authentic faith issues forth in righteous living. The message is grounded in soteriology—the saving work of Christ (vv. 5 and 8b). The cross means, among other things, that the human is freed for a life of righteousness and from a life alienated from

[48]Roberts, *The Letters of John*, 81-82.
[49]Kysar, *I, II, III John*, 22.
[50]*Ibid.*, 80.

God (i. e., sin). Furthermore, the cross means that humans have opportunity to be made children of God, if they choose to believe. Like the fourth evangelist, this author poses the alternatives dualistically—one is either a child of God or of the devil.[51]

The next section, 3:11-24, takes up the commandments that, if kept, enable the believers to avoid sin. In 3:23 John states, "And this is his commandment, that we should believe in the name of his Son Jesus Christ and love one another, just as he has commanded us" (1 John 3:23). In 3:11-24 he focuses upon loving one another. It is interesting that these are presented as one commandment, perhaps suggesting that the one who believes in Jesus without reservation in turn loves his brothers and sisters.

John now returns to what was from the beginning, "that we should love one another" (1 John 3:11). That which is from the beginning, in this case, has to do with the teaching of Christ and how that was emphasized when they first believed. I have often thought how crucial love is for the community of God's people, but how difficult it is for Christians to exhibit love for other church members, especially when they differ, let alone to love outsiders and enemies. Cain is now offered as the prime example of the hatred of one brother for another. The observation is that the murder was unjustified because Cain had an angry reaction over his own rejection and he took it out on his righteous brother. A long-time dispute has occurred over why Cain was unacceptable. Is it because he offered a cereal offering while Abel offered animal sacrifices? Later, both cereal and flesh offerings were required of the Israelites. John put the emphasis in Genesis more seemingly on the quality of Cain's life. "If you do well, will you not be accepted? And if you do not do well, sin is lurking at the door; its desire is for you, but you must master it" (Genesis 4:7). In 3:13 John mentions once again the hatred of the world for the believers. Power, greed, and lust prevail in the world. Love prevails for believers. Persons of the world have little toleration for those of another lifestyle.

Christians can be identified, not just for what they believe or what

[51]*Ibid.*, 82.

they talk about, but for what they do. How can one spot a Christian among myriads of persons? By observing whether they love one another. A Christian has passed from hatred, from darkness and death, into a new life of love for others. "We know that we have passed from death to life because we love one another" (1 John 3:13). The unbeliever is opposite. The one who does not love abides in death and does not exhibit the marks of eternal life.

How then can we see such love manifested concretely in believers? First, we see love exhibited in the final great act of our Lord on the cross. "We know love by this, that he laid down his life for us—and we ought to lay down our lives for one another" (1 John 3:16). What impressive steps Christians sometimes take when they see a sister or brother in need. Why do they reach out in such an unprecedented manner? One presumes they do it because of the extreme action of their Lord on their behalf. John thinks this should take a very concrete form. "How does God's love abide in anyone who has the world's goods and sees a brother or sister in need and yet refuses help?" (1 John 3:17).

Once in a Massachusetts church we had a family place membership that had moved to the Boston area from New Brunswick. The parents were undergoing trying times. The wife had mental problems and had been treated by psychiatrists and at a state hospital. The husband had had some difficulty finding suitable work and drove a refreshment van. He indicated to one of our members that he really needed about $2,000 to get their finances in order so they could move back to New Brunswick. Our member had a good steady position making concrete culverts, but his income was still inadequate because he had four children. His family lived frugally and drove an older automobile. He told me that he loaned this person the money because he had it and did not need it immediately. He said he would not worry about it if the family from New Brunswick never paid it back. Why did he do this? He took seriously the statement of John, "How does God's love abide in anyone who has the world's goods and sees a brother or sister in need and yet refuses to help?" (1 John 3:17).

In the 1970's we lived in Abilene, Texas. One Sunday I had an appointment to preach at a congregation in Austin. We started down on

Saturday afternoon, and shortly before we got to Brownwood, sixty miles to the south, the motor in our car starting making a terrible noise. I was almost certain it was a bad piston. I called Paul Wallace, now deceased, who was the preacher for a congregation there. I told him of the problem and asked him if he knew of anyone who could rent a car for us to drive on to Austin. I called him back after a time and he said that he hadn't found anyone who rented cars who would make them available on Saturday afternoon. He told me that I should drive to his house and he would lend me one of their cars. I told him that I was reluctant to accept his offer, but apparently I didn't have any alternative. So we gratefully drove to his house and went on to Austin. Since we weren't returning to Abilene until Monday, I called my dealer, who was a friend, and told him about the car. He said to put oil it and drive it back to Abilene, that the motor wouldn't be damaged more than it had been already. Considerable work had to be done on the motor because oil had leaked from the crankcase, of which I was unaware.

"Little children, let us love, not in word or speech, but in truth and action"(1 John 3:18). In the section 3:18-20, John takes up again the question as to how the believer can know she or he is walking in God's way. I think the reason he keeps coming back to certitude is because of the challenge of the secessionists. Their departure apparently caused several to question where they stood before God. John argues that truth is not merely a matter of focusing on the right issues and coming down on the right side. First, truth needs to be translated into action. By their action in departing, those who left indicated that they did not take their brothers and sisters seriously, much less love them. Those who act upon their love for their fellow believers have a sure ground for pushing aside doubt, should it arise. "And by this we will know that we are from the truth and will reassure our hearts before him whenever our hearts condemn us" (1 John 3:19-20).

John sees the heart as fragile and not always fully confident in respect to the believer's understanding and walk before God. Believers, however, do not need to constantly second-guess their walk if they are really grounded in the understanding of the Lord's way that they received from

John and the other teachers in the beginning of their journey. These beginning teachings are additionally confirmed by loving action. Confidence can further be gained through recognizing that God knows our hearts and is the one who finally makes the decision as to whether we are in the right. "God is greater than our hearts, and he knows everything" (1 John 3:20). Kysar, I think, adds an additional possible meaning.

> Hence, the author is saying that when our inner being judges against us, we are reassured by the fact that God is greater than our hearts and he knows everything. The sense of this obscure sentence is that God's grace and forgiveness exceed our inner state of being and God's knowledge measures us with greater generosity than we can measure ourselves.[52]

Because of the grace and mercy of our God, "we have boldness" before him, because our self-doubt fades when confronted by his mercy and grace. When we obey his commandments, centering in upon love for our fellows, "we receive from him whatever we ask" (1 John 3:22). His commands, as we noted previously, are that we should believe in the name of the Son Jesus Christ and love one another (1 John 3:23). Not only do we know that we do this by our commitment and our actions, but "by this we know that he abides in us, by the Spirit that he has given us" (1 John 3:24).

[52] *Ibid.*, 87.

chapter 7

TEST THE SPIRITS TO SEE WHETHER THEY ARE OF GOD 1 John 4:1-21

John has not as yet mentioned the Spirit explicitly, though "anointed by the Holy One" (1 John 2:20) may, if one considers the Gospel of John, imply the parakltos. The anointing in 2:7 also supplies teaching, as did the parakltos (John 14:26; 16:13). The first mention of the Spirit is in 1 John 3:24, in which the assurance that Christ abides in the believer is because of the presence of the Holy Spirit. As yet in the letter John has not mentioned that Christ abides in the believer, but in the Gospel this is so declared.

> The glory that you have given me I have given them, so that they may be one, as we are one, I in them and you in me, that they may become completely one, so that the world may know that you have sent me and have loved them even as you have loved me (John 17:22-23).

With the indwelling of the Holy Spirit as a backdrop, John feels compelled to comment on the characteristics of an authentic presence of the Holy Spirit. He apparently turns to this discussion regarding a discerning of the genuine Spirit because those who left also claimed to be anointed by the Spirit. Anyone can claim Holy Spirit anointment—then, down through the ages, and now! Does the fact that someone claims empowerment by the Holy Spirit make it the case? John does not think so. From what he sets out, it is clear he has concluded that those who left were not, in fact, anointed by the Holy Spirit. Their Docetic presuppositions about Christ and their secessionist action refute their claim. The test has been applied and the separatists failed the test. They were weighed in the balance and found wanting.

John lays out the necessity of examining every claim and not immediately accepting any at face value. "Beloved, do not believe every spirit, but test the spirits to see whether they are from God; for many false prophets have gone out into the world" (1 John 4:1). Notice how this parallels, "So now many antichrists have come" (1 John 2:18). How then can one test whether the spirit is from God? John provides two tests (1 John 4:2-6). The first is the right doctrine regarding Jesus Christ. The second is listening to the right source of teaching, which is either that of John himself or what all the Apostles taught from the beginning.

In 4:2-3 John sets forth the proper theology and the deviant one of those who left. The person who makes the true confession declares that Jesus Christ has come in the flesh (1 John 4:2). The person making this confession is from God, and this likewise confirms that the Spirit manifested is the Holy Spirit. The correct confession of Jesus is the first testing of the spirits. The person who will not confess Jesus is not from God. It seems fairly obvious what the latter claim is. However the specifics are to be worked out, it seems clear that those who departed separated Jesus the human from the Christ who occupied the body of Jesus. Once again John designates these the antichrist, as in 2:18. They promote an understanding of Jesus that makes him mere man, occupied by the Christ.

Those who left possessed a deviant Christology. They believed that Jesus, the man, was not God, even though the Christ inhabited him. They believed that God separated himself from humanity in Jesus. They therefore concluded that it is appropriate for them to separate themselves from those inferior believers who lacked special knowledge (gnosis) (1 John 2:21-22) and Holy Spirit anointment (1 John 2:20)—that is, to break *koinonia* (1 John 2:19). "Every spirit that confesses that Jesus Christ has come in the flesh is from God" (1 John 4:2). One must confess more than that Jesus came in the flesh. Those who left confessed as much. What they refused to confess was that Jesus was the Christ in the flesh. "Every Spirit that does not confess Jesus is not from God" (1 John 4:3). "Everyone who believes that Jesus is the Christ has been born of God" (1 John 5:1). The view John rejected may be that of Cerinthus, who lived in Asia Minor during John's declining years. Cerinthus believed that the Christ inhabited the man Jesus at his baptism. The Christ then departed from Jesus prior to his death on the cross. So the Christ was hermetically sealed off from the fleshly Jesus. In the view of the secessionists, God and the flesh are diametrically opposed. For John, the very Son of God is born as a human, enfleshed, or in later theological language, incarnate. Various Charismatic proclaimers these days declare that Jesus was a perfect man, but in no way was he in himself the divine Son of God. They do not make the confession called for by John.

Those who left obviously perceived themselves as spiritually superior because of their transcendent understanding of Christ that he by no means entered into the material of this world. This was in addition to their claim that they were enlightened in a far more enriching experience because of their special Spirit anointment. John assures those who remain that it is they who are truly of God, not the departed ones. "Little children, you are from God, and have conquered them" (1 John 4:4). It is rather the ones who remain who are God's beloved. Those who stayed are in God. Those who departed are in the world. That gives the faithful a privileged status, "for the one who is in you is greater than the one who is in the world" (1 John 4:4). Those who departed are from the world and the one who is in them is the evil one (1 John 3:8, 10, 12). "We know that we are the children of God, and that the whole world lies under the power of the evil one" (1 John 5:19). Those who left may make a great impression upon those outside the believing communities, but this is no sign that they have a superior relationship with God. They are of the world, therefore naturally the world listens to them (1 John 4:5). We live in at time in which numbers are often perceived of as the means of assessing where God is moving in the world. A rapidly expanding church is sometimes taken as the sign of God's unique blessing. According to John, acceptance by the majority of people is not the criterion for determining where God is at work. God's presence is signified by the correct understanding of Christ and the love of one believer for the other!

What additional test is needed to determine whether Christians authentically love or are involved in God's *koinonia*? The test John proposes for checking out the false prophets is determined by whether or not they will listen "to us." He wrote, "We are from God. Whoever knows God listens to us, and whoever is not from God does not listen to us. From this we know the spirit of truth and the spirit of error" (1 John 4:6). The question is why does John use we? Is this the editorial we of the writer and refers to John alone? Raymond Brown, as we saw, claimed that there was some sort of independent development of these churches and that they were unrelated to other streams of Christianity in the Ephesian region. The "we" therefore, to him, signifies the author of the document alone. C. H. Dodd, in contrast, identifies the "we" as the leading teachers of the whole church. Brown wrote,

> Dodd, *Epistles* 100, would argue that in his demand for listening "to us" the author refers to a "we" which stands for "The Church as a whole, speaking through its responsible teachers, who embody the authentic apostolic tradition." I find this quite unlikely on many scores. First, I John is concerned with the Johannine community and not with the "church as a whole"—a concept that is not attestedly Johannine. John 10:16 mentions that there are "other sheep" of Jesus but they are not part of "this fold," and so there is no evidence that a Johannine writer would have thought of his Community being in the same "church" as the other Christians.[53]

Brown provides two more reasons, but I find all of them rather con-

[53]Brown, *The Epistles of John*, 509. See C. H. Dodd, *The Johannine Epistles* (New York: Harper and Brothers, 1946) 100.

trived. I think that Brown is correct to contest the concept of the developed apostolic teaching that comes into vogue among the second-century writers. Nevertheless, I think that should Brown be wrong about the independence of the Johannine churches, as I think he is, then the "we" may indeed refer to the "from the beginning" teachings of the Apostles. Paul affirmed much earlier a common teaching of the Jerusalem leaders with which he and Barnabas concurred (Galatians 2:7-10. See also Acts 15).

In my judgment, therefore, a major way of checking out the teaching of various "false prophets," that is, testing the spirits whether they be of God, is to compare their teachings with those received from the beginning, that is, the apostolic teachings. What matters is whether the one who claims to be a teacher teaches the beginning apostolic message. At the time John wrote, these instructions may have been passed on orally. But the time is coming when they will be inscripturated in the New Testament. Should anyone therefore arrive with alleged Spirit-filled instructions, the test of their teachings is whether they conform to the apostolic teaching and way of life from the beginning. Roberts summed it up well when he wrote,

> The test of a prophet of God is not only that he recognizes that the Christ has appeared in the person of Jesus of Nazareth but that his teaching agrees with the essentials of faith and practice accepted by Christians from the beginning.[54]

John now returns to the subject of love. In a sense this is a continuation of the test for the bona fide teacher. First, the teacher must confess that Jesus Christ is the Son of God. Second, the instruction of the teacher must pass muster of those affirmations proclaimed at the beginning. Third, the teacher must not only proclaim love but likewise demonstrate *koinonia* in life's concrete activities. The separatists missed the mark on all counts and, perhaps most obviously, in their failure to love. The concrete indicator of their failure to love is the fact that they departed from the

[54]Roberts, *The Letters*, 110.

Johannine churches.

Love is from God. That is the center of his very being. Love likewise must be the *raison d'être* of the believer. "Beloved, let us love one another, because love is from God" (1 John 4:7). The departure from the children of God is a denial of God's love. God demonstrated his love concretely. "God sent his only Son into the world . . . to be the atoning sacrifice for our sin" (4:9-10). We are reminded of the much-quoted statement in John 3:16, "For God so loved the world that he gave his only Son, so that everyone who believes in him may not perish but may have eternal life." God is not a God who refrains from every contact with the material world that he has made. Rather, since his very being is love, he does not abstain from *koinonia* with everything he has made, including fleshy humanity made in his image. Love does not originate with humankind. It originates with God. It touches everything his hand has touched. And it likewise must be the passion of those who believe. "Beloved, since God loved us so much, we also ought to love one another" (1 John 4:11). God is transcendent to human life; nevertheless, his love penetrates the very being of humankind. "No one has ever seen God; if we love one another, God lives in us, and his love is perfected in us" (1 John 4:12). Believers do not need to see God if they concretely experience love among themselves. We are reminded of Paul's remark, "Hope does not disappoint us, because God's love has been poured into our hearts through the Holy Spirit that has been given to us" (Romans 5:5). In our time people constantly seek some ecstatic personal experience as a sign that God in interested in them as individuals. Both John and Paul propose an alternate way of discerning God's presence. When the body of Christ demonstrates deep and overpowering love for one another, then we truly know that God is present.

The love of God is present in the life of the believer for John, just as for Paul, because of the Spirit. "By this we know that we abide in him and he in us, because he has given us of his Spirit" (1 John 4:13). The author once again declares a personal, eye-witness knowledge of the Son. "And we have seen and do testify that the Father has sent his Son as the Savior of the world" (1 John 4:14). God's love is particular and visible in his very Son. In like manner, love in the body of Christ must be real, that is, it must be particular and visible. Jesus, Son of God, was born of woman God enfleshed. It is not enough that the believer confess, as did those who left, that Christ entered the world by dwelling in a human named Jesus. One must confess that the Son became flesh and dwelt among us full of grace and truth (John 1:14). "God abides in those who confess that Jesus is the Son of God" (1 John 4:15). John is not writing about God's love in the abstract. He is writing about the Son who became human and whom he heard, saw, and touched. He was the concrete demonstration of the love of God.

John reiterates, "God is love, and those who abide in love abide in God" (1 John 4:16). Now John enters a new dimension, that is, an eschatological one. He brought this up earlier in chapter 2. "And now, little children, abide in him, so that when he is revealed we may have confidence and not be put to shame before him at his coming" (1 John 2:28). Because love has been perfected in the believer, the outcome is that "we may have boldness on the day of judgment" (1 John 4:17). Furthermore, boldness is already possible in this world "because as he is, so are we in this world" (1 John 4:17). The "he" in this case apparently means Christ. If so, just as Christ's love was perfected in the world, so is the believers'. Roberts remarked,

> John's point is we are like Jesus Christ was, so we need not fear God's judgment. . . Jesus excelled in love, living in perfect harmony and subjection toward the Father and in deepest sympathy with man's needs and troubles. He faced the crisis of his own judgment so that, though he was innocent and was being punished as one guilty, love still showed through his action in complete freedom and confidence toward the Father. As he was, so are we. So, too, when our love has been perfected, sinful and human as we are, it is given to us through Christ to walk in the same confidence and assurance, even with the certainty of judgment day coming upon us.[55]

[55] *Ibid.*, 121.

As the result of their perfect love, the believers face the judgment with ultimate confidence, because there is no fear in love (1 John 4:18).

"God is love" (1 John 4:16). He, therefore, is the source of all love. All human love finds its source in him. In fact, believers are able to love, not because of resources of their own in the inner depth of their being, but because of God. "We love because he first loved us" (1 John 4:19). John returns now, I think, to the separatists. They apparently talked a lot about their boundless love for God and he for them. But John chides them, because he claims that by their action they have negated God's love. God's love leads to a reaching out to one's brother and sister. To depart sends the opposite message—hatred rather than love.

Those who say, "I love God," and hate their brothers or sisters, are liars; for those who do not love a brother or sister whom they have seen, cannot love God whom they have not seen (1 John 4:20).

Love must always take concrete form. God did not withhold himself, but in the Son he was heard, seen, and touched. Fellow humans likewise must exhibit a concrete reality so as to be heard, seen, and touched. While it is true, according to John, that no one has seen God, nevertheless, *koinonia* with God is brought to earth by the Son. "No one has ever seen God. It is God the only Son, who is close to the Father's heart, who has made him known" (John 1:18). The ultimate commandment that comes from God is that "those who love God must love their brothers and sisters also" (1 John 4:21).

chapter 8

DIVINE TESTIMONY AND THE TESTIMONY IN THE HEART
1 John 5:1-21

The first section of 1 John 5:1-5 reiterates much of what is stated in the later part of chapter 4. Despite what those who have left argued, John declares that being born of God necessitates a confession in regard to Jesus. "Everyone who believes that Jesus is the Christ has been born of God" (1 John 5:1). It is not enough to believe in a Docetic Christ who occupied the man Jesus. One must confess that the man Jesus is the Christ. This same declaration is made in 2 John.

> Many deceivers have gone out into the world, those who do not confess that Jesus Christ has come in the flesh; any such person is the deceiver and the antichrist! Be on your guard, so that you do not lose what we have worked for, but may receive a full reward. Everyone who does not abide in the teaching of Christ, but goes beyond it, does not have God; whoever abides in the teaching has both the Father and the Son (2 John 7-9).

Furthermore, as John wrote earlier (1 John 3:23) being born of God is clearly manifested in love for other believers. "Everyone who loves the parent loves the child" (1 John 5:1). Failing to enter into fellowship with other believers constitutes a failure to love. The new commandment is that believers must love one another. Those who left demonstrate hatred for their brothers and sisters, not love. The same point here is found in 2 John.

> But now, dear lady, I ask you, not as though I were writing you a new commandment, but one we have had from the beginning, let us love one another. And this is love, that we walk according to his commandments; this is the commandment just as you have heard it from the beginning you must walk in it (2 John 5-6).

It is clear that the love of God cannot be a personal relationship with God alone. The ecstatic experience in which one is lifted from the mundane world does not qualify. The love of God necessitates the love of the children of God (1 John 5:2). To love God entails obeying his commandments, and for John the love of brothers and sisters is always at the center of the commandments.

1 John in 5:3 introduces a new point regarding the commands of God. "And his commandments are not burdensome, for whatever is born of God conquers the world." It is not clear why God's commandments would be perceived as burdensome. Precedents for rules being burdensome, however, may be found in other parts of the New Testament. Jesus makes the point in Matthew that his expectations are light.

> Come to me, all you that are weary and are carrying heavy burdens, and I will give you rest. Take my yoke upon you, and learn from me; for I am gentle and humble in heart, and you will find rest for your souls. For my yoke is easy, and my burden is light (Matthew 11:28-30).

Paul also can depict the law as burdensome,

> And when you were dead in trespasses and the uncircumcision of your flesh, God made you alive together with him, when he forgave us all our trespasses, erasing the record that stood against us with its legal demands. He set this aside, nailing it to the cross

(Colossians 2:13-14).

It is not so clear, however, why John thinks that some perceive the commandments of God as burdensome. Kysar has a suggestion worthy of consideration,

> How might the commandments be viewed as burdensome? One wonders if the separatists, who practiced a freedom of moral obligation (cf. 2:9-11 above), might have declared such obligations a burden from which Christ had freed them (cf. Matt. 11:30). For the Christian the commandments are no burden, because they are obeyed with the context of love, which allows one to obey out of joy and gratitude rather than obligation.[56]

Clearly John believed that Christians have obligations and commandments. Christ brought a light burden, but not freedom from commandments. John does not agree with those who believe that the keeping of commandments is legalistic. The word legalism is often not employed in a New Testament manner. There legalism means making a rule a law of God when it is, in fact, a tradition of men (Mark 7), or asserting that keeping the law apart from faith is the way to salvation (Romans 9:32), or focusing on the letter of the law rather than the spirit of the law (Mark 2:23-28). John fully believed that Christians should obey the commandments, as did Paul (1 Corinthians 7:19). The "world" would indeed find the commandments burdensome, but not believers, "for whatever is born of God conquers the world" (1 John 5:4). The person born of God is a person of faith, and faith provides "the victory that conquers the world" (1 John 5:4). The one who believes that Jesus is the Son of God is a person of faith. That person is therefore born of God (1 John 5:5). The separatists believed that Christ is the Son of God, but not that Jesus is the Son of God. They, therefore, were neither persons of faith nor born of God.

The next section of 1 John, 5:6-13, presents testimony or evidence

---

[56]Kysar, *I, II, III John*, 105.

regarding Jesus as the Son of God. Jesus is Son because he came by water and blood (1 John 5:6). What then is the evidence, but perhaps more to the point, what does it prove? What it intends to prove, I believe, is clear, namely that Christ, who for John was identical with Jesus Christ, was truly human. The water and blood are material, earthly phenomena, and they came from the side of Jesus. Various views have been presented as that to which the water and blood pointed. J. W. Roberts believed they pointed to the water of the baptism of Jesus and his death.[57] Kysar believes this is a possibility. But he suggests a more natural explanation,

> That they are linked with John 19:34 ("But one of the soldiers pierced his side with a spear, and at once there came out blood and water") is clear; the author invokes that passage to prove the fleshly reality of God's revelation in Jesus.[58]

In addition to the water and blood testifying that it was Jesus the man who was the Christ, the Son of God, the Holy Spirit also testifies, and the Holy Spirit testifies to the truth. In the Gospel of John the Spirit (*paraklētos*) is identified with what is true.

This is the Spirit of truth, whom the world cannot receive, because it neither sees him nor knows him. You know him, because he abides with you, and he will be in you (John 14:17).

These three testify and all three agree (1 John 5:8). The King James Version reads for verses 5:7-8,

> For there are three that bear record in heaven, the Father, the Word, and the Holy Ghost: and these three are one. And there are three that bear witness in earth, the spirit, and the water, and the blood: and these three agree in one.

The KJV reading, however, is based upon later manuscripts. The

[57]Roberts, *Letters*, 131.
[58]Kysar, *I, II, III John*, 107.

NRSV reads, "There are three that testify: the Spirit and the water and the blood, and these three agree" (1 John 5:7-8). The part about three in heaven, Father, Word, and Holy Ghost, and the words depicting parallels on earth found in the KJV are deleted. Textual scholars label the deleted material in the modern translations the *Comma Johanneum*. According to Strecker, the *Comma* does not occur in essentially all the Greek texts dated before 1400. It is also absent from the Vetus Latina manuscripts before 600 and the Vulgate before 750.[59]

John argues that testimony is the key to who Jesus is. In the ancient world most people were aware of the presentation of testimony in law courts. John 5 draws upon this law court procedure. Testimony was commonly accepted as establishing or disproving a case. John proposes that if human testimony is admitted as relevant to the facts of a case, then even greater weight should be assigned to testimony from God. "If we receive human testimony, the testimony of God is greater" (1 John 5:9). God himself has testified. Those who have God's testimony have it in their hearts (1 John 5:10). In addition to the three exterior testimonies, "Those who believe in the Son of God have the testimony in their hearts" (1 John 5:10). Believers have assurances as to their involvement in the *koinonia* in which "the blood of Christ his Son cleanses us from all sin" (1 John 1:7), from heaven, from the witnesses who saw the actions of God in Christ, and "in their hearts" (1 John 5:10).

What is this witness in the heart? John does not elaborate. Roberts simply declares, "The testimony is no longer external but has become implanted in his heart and thus is there to reassure him."[60] While I think this statement is true as far as it goes, I think more can be said. Can this witness be the love found in the heart, which encourages those in *koinonia* to "lay down our lives for one another (1 John 3:16)?

> And by this we know that we are from the truth and will reassure our hearts before him whenever our hearts condemn us; for God

[59]Strecker, *The Johannine Letters*, 188-191.
[60]Roberts, *The Letters*, 134.

> is greater than our hearts, and he knows everything. Beloved, if our hearts do not condemn us, we have boldness before God; and we receive from him whatever we ask, because we obey his commandments and do what pleases him (1 John 3:19-22).

The believers know that they have committed their lives to God. They know, therefore, by how they act whether or not they are showing the love that is concomitant with that commitment. The testimony within is not, as in a number of religious traditions, simply a warm, heartfelt assurance. The believer knows by whether or not the results specified by John accrue in lived existence before God and fellow believers.

Failure to believe, according to John, is to designate God a liar, because if one believes that when God speaks, he speaks the truth, then not believing shows disdain for the divine testimony. The testimony of God is that he will give eternal life to those who believe in Jesus Christ (1 John 5:11). That life is in the Son. According to the Gospel of John, "What has come into being in him was life, and the life was the light of all people" (John 1:3-4). Those who have the Son have life, while those who do not have him do not have life. Now John concludes, "I write these things to you who believe in the name of the Son of God, so that you may know you have eternal life" (1 John 5:13). We are reminded of the statement in the Gospel,

> Now Jesus did many other signs in the presence of his disciples, which are not written in this book. But these are written so that you may come to believe that Jesus is the Messiah, the Son of God, and that through believing you may have life in his name (John 20:30-31).

The difference is that in the letters no effort is made to present signs. Rather the emphasis is upon the witnesses. Witnesses often are critical as the ground for belief in the Gospel also, for example, John 5:31-47.

John returns now to the matter of boldness (see earlier 1 John 3:20; 4:17). Believers can be bold, John declares, because whatever they ask for that is in accordance with his will, God will hear. If they know in advance that he will hear and that he gives whatever is requested, then they know that the request will be granted (1 John 5:15). Exactly how the will is determined is not declared, but presumably the commandments to confess Jesus Christ and love the brothers and sisters provide a clue.

The next verses, 5:16-17, likely have received more comments than any other statements in 1 John. John first declares that if anyone sees a believer committing a sin that is not mortal, or unto death (which is stark but, I think, the better translation), they may pray for the sinner and God will forgive, that is, "give life to" such a one. But there is a sin that is mortal, that is, a sin unto death. John recommends that they not pray about the sin unto death. Presumably, the point is that it is senseless to pray about the sin unto death, for God will not forgive the person who has committed a sin unto death; that's why the sin is so deathly. John clarifies further by declaring that all sin is wrong; however, there are sins that are not unto death. The age-old question is what is the difference between a sin that is unto death and one that is not? The additional question is why should one not pray for the sin unto death?

It is wise to focus on the sin unto death because to do so also defines other sins, that is, those which are not sins unto death and are forgivable. Various proposals have been made, for example, that the sin unto death is a severe sin, such as murder or sexual perversion, the penalty for which may be death. Another proposal is that it is a sin for which the church may assign death, such as the deceit of Ananias and Sapphira in Acts 5. A third possibility is that it is a sin so despicable that the church sets out to withdraw fellowship or excommunication, for example, Julian the Apostate (A. D. 332-363) offering sacrifices in pagan temples. Still others have equated the sin unto death with blasphemy against the Holy Spirit, as presented in Mark 3:28-30. In the Gospel of John, it may be pointed out that the rejection of Jesus as the one sent by God is an unforgivable sin. "I told you that you would die in your sins, for you will die in your sins unless you believe that I am he" (John 8:24).

Rensberger has identified, in my opinion, the proper focus regarding this unforgivable sin.

> Thus, the deadly sin may be the opponents' christological denial, which in its way is also a rejection of God. There is another factor as well, however. The only other mention of death in 1 John is at 3:14-15, where failure to love one's brother or sister leaves one abiding in death rather than life. This failure is thus also part of the "sin that leads to death." It includes breaking fellowship with the community in which alone life is to be found. . . Thus, the " sin that leads to death" is probably a lack of christological faith and lack of love taken together, since precisely this lack cuts one off from eternal life.[61]

As I wrote at the start of this book, fellowship (*koinonia*) is the critical issue in 1 John. But it is not simply the question of whether one has cut themselves off from the community of the faithful, but the reason for doing so. I have argued that those who left the churches in 1 John held God to be self-contained in a transcendent world and ontologically unable to enter into material reality, much less have fellowship with the created order and humans in it. Since God himself is of this character, his Son likewise cannot enter in any real sense into physical reality. Christ the Son entered into the man Jesus when he had already attained adulthood, and departed before the death of Jesus on the cross. Therefore, we might say that though the Son was upon the earth, he was hermetically sealed off from it and, therefore, by no means contaminated with flesh and blood. From these convictions, it followed for the secessionists that since they too had been anointed with the Spirit of God, they too in soul were transcendent from flesh and blood. Since God does not enter into fellowship with his world, there was no need for them to remain in fellowship with those who had not attained their enlightened state.

John's views are opposite to these. At the beginning of the letter he charged that God fellowshipped and loved the world he created, especially humankind in this world. Furthermore, his Son came as a human. His body was material and human blood coursed through his veins. God

[61]Rensberger, *I, II, III John*, 140.

and Jesus Christ the Son loved the world, and Jesus died for the world. The sin unto death is, therefore, to conceive of God and his Son as sealed off from the world of humankind. They do not, in fact, love the world, nor are they in fellowship with it. I first came to think this way about the sin unto death through reading the Epistle and Willi Marxson's *Introduction to the New Testament*. He put the point succinctly, "He who cuts himself off from the Church commits the 'sin unto death (v. 16).'"[62]

It is now possible to comment on the statements about prayer. The believers should feel free to pray for any sins they see their brothers and sisters committing except for the sin unto death. The reason is apparent. These brothers and sisters are in fellowship with the church, and John has already declared that the blood of Jesus Christ removes all sins for those who faithfully remain in the church. "For if we walk in the light as he himself is in the light, we have fellowship with one another, and the blood of Jesus his Son cleanses us from all sin" (1 John 1:7). All of the sins of those in the fellowship of the body of Christ may be forgiven. But, "there is a sin that is mortal; I do not say that you should pray about that" (1 John 5:16). In other words, John says, don't pray for those who left the church, such as, "Father, forgive them for leaving us." The separatists are no longer in the place where sins are being forgiven, that is, in the body of the believers that remain. It might be appropriate to pray that "they come to their senses and return." But is appears that John thinks their departure is permanent, and they will not return, regardless of how many prayers might be uttered.

Sin is a human condition that alienates believers from God. Sin cannot be swept under the rug (1 John 5:17). Only God in his Son is able to address it. Believers who are born of God are out of the reach of sin as long as they stay in church and keep the commandments of Christ. "God protects them, and the evil one does not touch them" (1 John 5:18). But sometimes believers in the church permit that barrier to break down, and they do in fact sin. In that case, "he is the atoning sacrifice for our sins" (1 John 2:2). Believers are readily aware of the contrast between those who are born of God and of the world. "The whole world lies under the

[62]Willi Marxsen, *Introduction to the New Testament*, trans. G. Buswell (Philadelphia: Fortress Press, 1968) 263.

power of the evil one" (1 John 5:19). Those who are born of God know that the Son has come and they know who it is that is true—that is God's Son, Jesus Christ. "He is the true God and eternal life" (1 John 5:20). We are reminded immediately of the opening of John's Gospel.

> In the beginning was the Word, and the Word was with God, and the Word was God. He was in the beginning with God. All things came into being through him, and without him not one thing came into being (John 1:1-3).

The Epistle abruptly comes to a close without the usual epistolary ending and in somewhat of a puzzle. "Little children, keep yourselves from idols." About this Kysar wrote,

> In keeping with the context it seems our author levels one last blast at the opponents, charging them with the most serious of offenses against God—idolatry. He regards their infatuation with their own views as a kind of idolatry. They have made idols of their own doctrines and have pursued them with a dogmatism which has split the community.[63]

In conclusion we may judge the Epistle as successful in instilling in the readers the confidence that they are headed in the right direction and should stay the course. It's the people who have left, who exuded a superior confidence that their anointment and understanding of God placed them head and shoulders above the remaining pew sitters, who are in trouble with God. The remaining believers should be bold in their affirmation that the Son of God became fully human and, therefore, in complete *koinonia* with those who believe in him, love him, and keep his commandments. It is they who walk with their heads up before God, for they walk in his light, "and the blood of Jesus his Son cleanses [them] from all sin."

---

[63]Kysar, *I, II, III John*, 118.

chapter 9

THE MESSAGE OF 1 JOHN FOR THE TWENTY-FIRST CENTURY

The first Letter of John to the Christians around Ephesus was the word of God for churches of the region in the first century. 1 John is still the word of God to Christians around the world in these early years of the third millennium *anno domini*, that is, 2,000-plus years since the birth of Jesus Christ. The message of the letter is as relevant today for our social-religious location as it was nineteen hundred years ago, and perhaps even more so. If many antichrists went out into the world late in the first century, many more have gone out into the world in the early years of the twenty-first century. If theologies that departed from the beginning Christian message already were raising their standards in the first century, how much more so in the twenty-first? A number of years ago the Coca Cola Bottling Company, in an effort to capture a new clientele in a changing time, decided to market the "New Coke." They thought it wise to retain the "Classic Coke." The "New Coke" did not do well, and soon the company abandoned it for the old or classic Coke and dropped classic off the bottle. It was John's hope that the threatened Christians of his circle would reject the new and cling to that "classic" teaching they received from the beginning. They needed to stay the course.

It is clear from the Letter that John believed that God is active in the human world as Father (1 John 1:2, 2:22, 3:1, 4:14), Son (1:3, 2:22, 3:23, 4:9) and Spirit (3:24, 4:13, 5:6). The Godhead is a Trinity of revelation.

The fourth-century church fathers, Basil the Great, Gregory Nazianzus, Gregory of Nyssa, and Athanasius, may have cast the Trinity into a Greek metaphysical ontology which is not that biblical, that is, that God is one in essence, but three in persons. Nevertheless, it is undeniable in John and other New Testament writers that God revealed himself in a threefold manner, as Father, Son, and Spirit. Consider, for instance, Paul's benediction in 2 Corinthians 13:14, "The grace of the Lord Jesus Christ, the love of God, and the communion of the Holy Spirit be with all of you." Another clear example is our Lord's command in Matthew 28:19, "Go therefore and make disciples of all nations, baptizing them in the name of the Father and of the Son and of the Holy Spirit."

According to John one should be committed to the version of the faith taught in the beginning, "the message you have heard from the beginning" (1 John 3:11). For him, the accepting of each "person" of the Godhead, the Father, the Son, and Spirit, is a theological imperative. Much theological confusion reigns in the contemporary world because the three are not consistently affirmed.

God

It is still the case that some affirm a transcendent God who shuns every contact with the affairs of humankind. In the fourth century A. D., Arius questioned whether it was possible for the transcendent Father to enter time and history. He therefore declared that the Son was divine, but subordinate to the Father. He was not with God from the beginning, as John wrote (John 1:1; 1 John 2:13); rather, there was a time when he was not. William Ellery Channing (1780-1842), sometimes called the father of American Unitarianism, claimed a similar position, namely that Jesus was the Son of God, divine, but not God himself. Ralph Waldo Emerson (1803-1882), Harvard graduate and for a time a Unitarian minister, finally took this one step farther and declared that although Jesus possessed a spark of the divine and was an extraordinary person, he was not divine. His views, shared by the famous Unitarian Minister Theodore Parker (1810-1860), were designated Transcendentalism. Humans themselves, they declared, likewise possess this same spark or over-soul from God.

Contemporary Unitarians are various, but tend to be humanistic, some not even professing a conviction about God.

Beginning late in the nineteenth century, many continental and a few American scholars declared God to be beyond space and time and uninvolved in the affairs of humankind. One of the best known of these was the German church historian Adolf Harnack (1851-1930). He heralded the Fatherhood of God, the brotherhood of man, and the infinite value of the human soul, but eschewed divine Sonship for Jesus. Rudolf Bultmann (1884-1976), the foremost German New Testament scholar of the twentieth century, held that the importance of Jesus was that he heralded faith as the unique feature of human existence. But Jesus was not divine. He said that modern man must hold a scientific view of reality, that all causes in this world are this worldly. This rules out miracles and any manner in which God influences the physical universe or any beings in it. For him the value of any message from the Scripture resided not in the God of the Old Testament, but in Jesus of the New. This was because Bultmann argued that Jesus embraced the existentialist view that to be human is to exist as a "being there," that is, having faith in a goal not yet attained. For him, authentic existence only occurs when by faith we live out a future vision of what we want to be. What is wrong with the conclusion that Jesus is less than God? According to John, if this is true, humans are still bogged down in sin.

But if anyone does sin we have an advocate with the Father, Jesus Christ the righteous, and he is the atoning sacrifice for our sins, and not for ours only but for the sins of the whole world" (1 John 2:1-2).

"The Son of God was revealed for this purpose, to destroy the works of the devil" (1 John 3:8). It is only the God of the universe himself who is able to address the mystery and catastrophe of human sin, for non-earthly phenomena are involved in its propagation.

Christ

Another stream of thought that has some current outcropping is a focus on Jesus almost to the exclusion of God. It is interesting that in this letter God (56 times) or Father (12 times) appears more frequently than the Son

(21 times), Jesus Christ (6 times), Jesus is the Christ (2 times), or Jesus alone (4 times). The same frequency is true throughout the New Testament. In medieval times, in some Roman Catholic orders a dedication to the passion of Christ, that is, his suffering, brought a special focus on Jesus. A case in point is the work of Ann Catherine Emmerich, *The Dolorous Passion of Our Lord Jesus Christ* that influenced Mel Gibson's *The Passion of the Christ*. In the nineteenth-century British and American hymn tradition, many more hymns focused on Christ than on God. If hymns are the main source of some people's theology, this likewise is a misplaced emphasis from the standpoint of John. While many hymns may be mentioned, three that come to mind are "Tell It to Jesus Alone," "Blessed Assurance Jesus Is Mine," and "I Come to the Garden Alone," which has the refrain regarding the Son, "And he walks with me and he talks with me."

In the late 1960's the Jesus movement erupted in conjunction with counter-culture developments.

> By the late-1960's, the youth counter-culture had reached its peak. Drug use flourished, "hippies" were the center of attention, and most striking of all, significant numbers of these youth were becoming Christians. Onlookers knew these young people by various names: "Jesus Freaks," "Jesus People," and "Street Christians." A large proportion of these youthful evangelists for Jesus were only a short while removed from drugs, "free love," and alienation from "straight society." They spoke of a "Jesus Revolution" and believed that the endtimes were near (Enroth:12).
>
> Most adhered to the "fundamentals of the faith," doctrines outlining a faith of biblical inerrancy, and affirmed fundamental Christian views. On the whole, the primary focus of the Movement centered on salvation through an "experience of faith in Jesus Christ" (DiSabatino, 1999:5).[64]

[64]www.religiousmovements.lib.virginia.edu.

Actually in their statements of faith some of these groups affirmed an allegiance to the doctrine of the Trinity. But their focus obviously was on Christ, not on God.

Another focus more on Jesus than on God happened in the world of scholarship, not only in the case of the New Testament scholar Rudolf Bultmann, but with the greatest theologian of the twentieth century, Karl Barth (1886-1968) of the University of Basel in Switzerland. Perhaps the often-told story points to his focus upon Jesus Christ. Barth gave a speech in Chicago, mostly to seminary professors and students. When asked by a student what to him is the most profound theological thought, Barth replied, "Jesus loves me, this I know, for the Bible tells me so." My Old Testament professor at Harvard was particularly exercised over the theology of Barth and labeled it "Christomonism."[65] Wright was especially concerned because he was convinced that the Old Testament was crucial for the understanding of God, the Father of the Lord Jesus Christ. Certain Old Testament theologians influenced by Barth had taken the position that what the Old Testament means theologically almost altogether points to Jesus Christ. Two that come to mind are Walter Vischer, *The Witness of the Old Testament to Christ* (SCM, 1949) and G. A. F. Knight, *A Christian Theology of the Old Testament* (John Knox, 1959). But Wright was also concerned because he believed that the move by Barth was some effort to avoid the charge of Kant that God is beyond human experience and knowledge, but Jesus Christ has entered the realm of human experience and therefore can alone be the focus of theology.

It's not that Barth ignored God. He devoted a volume of his famous *Church Dogmatics* to God; nevertheless, the center point for his theology was Christ. Paul McGlassen wrote,

> Barth's biblical interpretation, like his theology generally, exhibits a christological focus. Biblical texts are to be brought into relation to the person of Jesus Christ, or rather are to be seen in this, their true light. Christocentric exegesis is characteristic

[65]G. Ernest Wright, *The Old Testament and Theology* (New York: Harper & Row, 1969) 13-38.

> of B.'s exegesis of the NT as of the OT; whatever historical relation the NT writings may be thought to bear to the historical figure of Jesus is irrelevant to the problem of finding in them a real witness for Jesus Christ.[66]

Why is the main focus on Jesus Christ problematic? In 1 John it is clear that eternal life resides with the Father and was revealed and made possible by the Lord Jesus Christ (1 John 1:2-3). The fellowship of the believer is not uniquely with Christ but with the Father and the Son. "And truly our fellowship is with the Father and with his Son Jesus Christ" (1 John 1:4). The believers are called to "abide in the Son and in the Father" (1 John 2:24). Believers are charged to love God and keep his commandments (1 John 5:2). Clearly, for John, the identity of the true God is that he is the Father of the Lord Jesus Christ. To affirm what was taught from the beginning, we need to emphasize the Father and the Son and the Spirit!

The Spirit

In our time, however, if any member of the Godhead has received special emphasis it is the Holy Spirit. This has come about in part because of the great outburst of the neo-Charismatic movement beginning with Dennis Bennett of St. Mark's Episcopal Church in Van Nuys, California, in 1959. In a few years this movement spread throughout the United States among both Protestants and Roman Catholics. The original Pentecostals, starting with Charles Parham (1873-1929) in Topeka, Kansas, in 1900, and given a new thrust under the ministry of William J. Seymour (1870-1922) at the Azusa Street Mission in Los Angeles in 1906, were also reinvigorated by the movement. Some claim that at the beginning of the twenty-first century more than half of all Christians in the world are Charismatic. Others place the numbers toward a third. Regardless, Charismatics are a significant force in contemporary

[66]Paul McGasson, "Karl Barth," *The Dictionary of Biblical Interpretation*, John H. Hays, ed. (Nashville: Abingdon Press, 1999) I:100.

Christendom. In these circles the Holy Spirit is upstage center. God's salvific work in the world is through the Holy Spirit.

Not all Charismatics go to the extreme of Benny Hinn (1953-), but his perspective, in effect, subsumes the Father and the Son under the category of the Spirit. Hinn has two daily television programs on various networks and stations, "This is Your Day!" and "Manna from Heaven." He holds religious crusades around the world. He has come under constant criticism from a number of sources; nevertheless, he apparently thrives and secures adequate funds for all his enterprises. Hinn was born in Jaffa of Greek-Armenian heritage. His family moved to Toronto. He attributed his conversion and encouragement to ministry as the result of attending a crusade of Kathleen Kuhlman in Pittsburgh, Pennsylvania, and his talks with her. Hinn has made differing statements, but he sometimes presents the Holy Spirit as the true manifestation of God and, if not replacing the Father, at least identical with him. The Spirit is all and does all as Hinn proclaims at least some of the time. In view of the affirmations regarding the Spirit, both the Son and Father recede into the far distance. It is not clear to me what role the death of Jesus plays in his theology, if any. He has said that Jesus is the perfect man and is not divine.

The Holy Spirit is not the focal point in 1 John; nevertheless, he has a very important role. In 1 John, the Father is the focus regarding larger reality, the Son is the central point regarding the forgiveness of sins, and the Holy Spirit is focal point of the believers' knowledge of the ways of God. The Spirit is mentioned seven times in 1 John (2:20, 3:24, 4:13, 5:8), and anointing of the Spirit is mentioned twice (2:20, 27). The believers know that God abides in them and that they abide in God because of the Spirit. "All who obey his commandments abide in him, and he abides in them. And by this we know that he abides in us, by the Spirit that he has given us" (1 John 3:24). The way the believers know of the inner presence of the Spirit, according to 1 John, is not so much from an inner feeling or ecstatic moment, but because of the manifestations of the Spirit in their lives. They possess knowledge (1 John 2:20). They love their fellow believers and keep God's commandments (1 John 3:24; 4:13). The Spirit also testifies that Jesus is the Christ, the Son of God (1 John 5:6, 8).

We live in a time in which in various quarters there is a misplaced emphasis upon the Spirit. The Spirit is perceived in the Gnostic manner as non-material and not actually partaking of material reality. If the Spirit is God and the Spirit accomplishes all, then God is exonerated from direct contact with the material world in which humans live. But the Son of God came as fully human. Human liquids and blood flowed from his side on the cross (1 John 5:6). Redemption and forgiveness of sins was achieved through his physical death. "The blood of Jesus his Son cleanses us from all sin" (1 John 1:7). The fellowship with God is not some ephemeral spirit fellowship. God was heard, seen, and touched in the flesh in the Son, Jesus Christ, who was fully human (1 John 1:1-4). God in the life of the believer is concretely manifested in the material world through the very physical water of baptism. God is praised through acts in the material world he created. We exhibit our love for our fellows through concrete material objects, that is, the "world's goods" (1 John 3:17). The Gnostic conception of a transcendental Spirit God is rampant in our time. Harold Bloom, the renowned Yale Professor, in his book *American Religion: The Emergence of the Post-Christian Nation* (1992), has charged that "America is a nation of Gnostics, believers in a pre-Christian tradition of individual divinity." He offers as two main examples Southern Baptists and Mormons.

The Church

It may be that the most important message for our time from 1 John has to do with the church. I might first of all observe that I am under no illusion regarding the differences in the twenty-first century as compared with the first in regard to churches that profess to be Christian. In the context of 1 John there were at best two different groups professing to be Christians, the circles of churches around John, and those formed by the people who departed. In our time, according to one report there are above 1,500 Christian faith groups in America. So exactly what 1 John might mean in such a complex plethora of different churches may be difficult to determine.

1 John, however, provides certain central affirmations about the church that are critical. First, Christian involvement in the church is

imperative if one pursues original Christian guidelines as John recommends. "Let what you heard from the beginning abide in you. If what you heard from the beginning abides in you, then you will abide in the Son and in the Father" (1 John 2:24). God in his Son Jesus Christ entered the world so as to bring people into fellowship (*koinonia*) with themselves (1 John 4:1-4). Jesus entered into *koinonia* with the first believers, and they in turn wished to share that *koinonia* with all who will believe (1 John 1:3). Those who come to believe through the apostolic witness are in turn to be in loving fellowship with others. From 1 John, I argue it is not possible to be a good Christian and not be church-involved. That is, for John, a contradiction of terms. "We know love by this, that he laid down his life for us—and we ought to lay down our lives for one another" (1 John 3:16). A Christian is involved deeply in a community faith. For John it makes no sense whatsoever to say, "Jesus, Yes!"—"the church, No!"

Second, every believer, though constantly seeking to avoid sin, nevertheless fails. "If we say that we have not sinned, we make him a liar, and his word is not in us" (1 John 1:9). Jesus Christ himself is the "atoning sacrifice for our sins" (1 John 2:2). But his atoning sacrifice only has efficacy if one is involved with a body of Christian believers. "But if we walk in the light as he himself is in the light, we have fellowship with one another, and the blood of Jesus his Son cleanses us from all sin" (1 John 1:7). The plain conclusion of John's affirmation is that those outside the church are no longer receiving forgiveness of sin. They are not benefiting from the blood of Christ that was shed for those who believe alone. From 1 John we can say that there is no forgiveness of sin outside the church. The church administers the forgiveness of sin, not through its officials, not through a democratic vote of the church, but through the love and fellowship shared by the body of believers.

Third, leaving the church is not a God-recommended option. In our time people constantly leave churches and they perceive it as their God-given privilege. They pride themselves in their courage to protest with the feet. Departing from churches because of not being fed by the preaching, not being uplifted by the music, or not finding compatible members is often seen as the sign of whether one is a dedicated Christian. Very few people seem to be commending staying put these days. A common perception seems to be that it's only lifeless, conventional, half-hearted Christians who work in the same church year after year. John praises those who stay and excoriates those who leave.

> Those who say, "I love God," and hate their brothers or sisters, are liars; for those who do not love a brother or sister whom they have seen, cannot love God whom they have not seen. The commandment we have from him is this: those who love God must love their brothers and sisters also (1 John 4:20-21).

I don't know how to sort out every specific case as to whether one should stay or leave. I do think, however, that what John has written should give us serious pause. According to him, it is better for us to stay and lift up our weak and lethargic brothers and sisters, than to depart.

I therefore close with what I consider to be the most powerful line in 1 John.

> If we say that we have fellowship with him while we are walking in darkness, we lie and do not do what is true; but if we walk in the light as he himself is in the light, we have fellowship with one another, and the blood of Jesus his Son cleanses us from all sin (1 John 1:6-7).

annotated bibliography
OF SELECTED COMMENTARIES

Black, C. Clifton, "The First, Second, and Third Letters of John," *New Interpreter's Bible* (Nashville: Abingdon Press, 1998). This commentary is written by a professor of New Testament at the Princeton Theological Seminary. Black believes the backgrounds are more Hellenistic Judaism than Gnostic, thus reflecting the move away from earlier views, especially that of Bultmann, that the backgrounds are Gnostic. Black does an excellent job of placing statements within the context of both the Gospel and the Epistles. He brings to bear not only the views of the contemporary scholars, but also those of Calvin, Wesley, and others from the history of the interpretation of these letters. The commentary contains "Reflections" for how the message of the letter may find meaning in the contemporary world.

Brown, Raymond C., *The Community of the Beloved Disciple* (New York: Paulist Press, 1979). Raymond Brown is among the major interpreters of the Gospel and the Epistles of John in the twentieth century. Brown is Roman Catholic and taught at Union Theological Seminary in New York, as well as at various Roman Catholic Seminaries in both the United States and in Rome. In this book Brown sets fourth the manner in which he understands the origins of what he designates the "Johannine Community" or the "Community of the Beloved Disciple," referring to the disciple Jesus loved, a phrase found only in the Gospel of John. He sets out four stages in the development of the Johannnine churches which he perceives as struggles with the world, with the Jews, and with other Christians, and finally within the community itself. This is a major work, often cited.

Brown, Raymond C., *The Epistles of John* (Garden City, NY: Doubleday, 1982). As with Brown's two-volume commentary on the Gospel of John, this commentary of eight hundred pages is a thorough and systematic reflection upon the three Epistles. While Brown may not always be correct in the positions he takes upon the Epistles, his comments are always worth reading.

Bruce, F. F., *The Epistles of John: Introduction, Exposition, and Notes* (Grand Rapids: Eerdmans, 1979). Bruce was a major British scholar at the University of Manchester to whom, especially, Neo-Evangelical New Testament scholars have been indebted. His commentary provides excellent backgrounds and insights from a basically conservative perspective.

Bultmann, Rudolf, *The Johannine Epistles* (Philadelphia: Fortress Press, 1973). Rudolf Bultmann, a major German scholar in the twentieth century at the University of Marburg, has written major commentaries on both the Gospel of John and the Johannine Epistles. As he did with the Gospel, Bultmann questioned the literary unity of 1 John and found an early version of the Letter which the final author, not John the Apostle, incorporated. Bultmann located the background for the Epistle in Gnostic dualism and a Docetism like that of Cerinthus. Despite questionable beginning points, Bultmann has interesting reflections on the controversial materials in the letter.

Coffman, James Burton, *Commentary on James, 1 & 2 Peter, 1, 2, & 3 John, Jude* (Austin: Firm Foundation Pub. House, 1979). Burton Coffman, a Churches of Christ minister who recently reached the one hundred year milestone, has published a series of commentaries on the whole Bible. His observations are always conservative, he reports on the conclusions of the older, well known English-speaking commentators, for example, Henry, Clark, and Barnes, and is helpful in some cases with homiletic observations.

Dodd, C. H., *The Johannine Epistles* (New York: Harper and Brothers, 1946). Dodd, one of the major British New Testament scholars at Cambridge University in the twentieth century, published widely on the Gospel of John, though not a major commentary. His commentary on the Epistles provides solid background materials and is a lucid and judicial exposition of the text.

Edwards, Ruth B., *The Johannine Epistles* (Sheffield: Sheffield Academic Press, 1996). Edwards, a British scholar, commenced by suggesting that the elect lady in 2 John was in charge of a church or churches. She proposes that the letters are not so much polemical, but focused upon the need for the believers to manifest the love of God in their fellowship.

Houlden, J. L. A *Commentary on the Johannine Epistles* (London: A. & C. Black, 1994). Houlden was a New Testament professor at Oxford University in England. Houlden doubts that the author was the Apostle John, but thinks he may have been the Elder John in Ephesus, mentioned by Papias and Irenaeus. He sees the letters as addressing the dissidence generated by the differing views on the incarnation of the Messiah in the man Jesus. He has many helpful observations in the commentary.

Kysar, Robert, *I, II, III John* (Minneapolis: Augsburg, 1986). Kysar, now at Emory University, has been at the forefront of American Johannine studies. This is a helpful commentary that I have constantly consulted for this book.

Lieu, Judith M., *The Theology of the Johannine Epistles* (Cambridge: Cambridge University Press, 1991). Lieu is a lecturer at King's College, London. This book focuses upon the theological centers of the Johannine Epistles. Her observations begin from the theological language in the Epistles. She situates the Epistle in the New Testament and makes observations on its contemporary use.

Loader, William, *The Johannine Epistles* (London: Epworth Press, 1992). This is a short commentary, but it has many helpful insights. Professor Loader is a professor at Murdock University in Perth, Australia.

Marshall, I. Howard, *The Epistles of John* (Grand Rapids: Eerdmans, 1978). Marshall is a well known, basically conservative scholar at the University of Aberdeen in Scotland. This commentary offers considerable detailed insight of a traditional nature.

O'Day, Gail R., "1, 2, and 3 John," *The Women's Bible Commentary*, eds. C. A. Newsom and S. H. Ringe, (Louisville: Westminster/John Knox, 1992). O'Day, who teaches at the Chandler School of Theology at Emory University, has developed considerable expertise on the Johannine Literature. Though relatively short, this commentary has many valuable suggestions.

Perkins, Pheme, *Epistles of John* (Wilmington, Del.: M. Glazier, 1984). Perkins is a professor at Boston College and is Roman Catholic. This is a more popularly focused commentary in a New Testament series and represents competent scholarship.

Rensberger, David, *1 John, 2 John, 3 John* (Nashville: Abingdon Press, 1997). Rensberger is a professor at the Interdenominational Theological Center in Atlanta. This recent commentary comprises judicious reflection upon the Johannine Epistles. Rensberger has worked extensively in the major recent commentators. One has to read slowly and carefully in this commentary because of the density of the reflections, but it is short. I find myself agreeing more with Rensberger than any other commentator. He is especially helpful in regard to the theological arguments in the Epistle.

Roberts, J. W., *The Letters of John* (Austin: R. B. Sweet, 1968). Roberts was a professor of New Testament at Abilene Christian University. He was especially interested in Greek meanings and early

Christian history. He writes in a straight-forward manner and this commentary can be very helpful in clarifying difficult passages.

Schnackenburg, Rudolf, *The Johannine Epistles: Introduction and Commentary* (NewYork: Crossroad, 1992). Professor Schnackenburg has been a major interpreter of the Gospel of John and the Johannine Epistles. He retired from the Roman Catholic faculty of the University of Würzburg in Germany. This is a significant commentary worthy of constant consulting. Snackenburg does an excellent job of placing his observations within the context of contemporary Johannine studies.

Smalley, S. S., *1, 2, 3 John* (Waco: Word Books, 1984). Smalley, an Anglican scholar, has written a major commentary that is basically conservative. He examines regularly the Greek text. This is a worthwhile commentary to consult.

Smith, D. Moody, *First, Second, and Third John* (Louisville: John Knox, 1991). Moody, professor of New Testament at the Duke University Divinity School, has been a major interpreter of the Johannine literature in America. His work, therefore, is noteworthy in an expression of judicious comments on the text of 1 John.

Strecker, Georg, *The Johannine Letters* (Minneapolis: Fortress Press, 1996). Strecker was professor of New Testament at the University of Göttingen. His major advisor for his Ph.D. was Rudolf Bultmann at the University of Marburg. This is a translation of a major German commentary and represents a significant addition to commentaries on the Johannine Epistles.

Thompson, Marianne Meye, *1, 2, 3 John* (Downer's Grove: InterVarsity Press, 1992). Thompson is a professor of New Testament at Fuller Theological Seminary. This commentary is a useful guide to 1 John and is helpful for preaching insights.

Wilder, Amos N., "The First, Second, and Third Epistles of John," *New Interpreter's Bible* (Nashville: Abingdon Press, 1957). Wilder was professor of New Testament at Harvard Divinity School and the person from whom I took Introduction to the New Testament. This is a solid, judicious commentary.

Womack, Morris, *I, II, III John* (Joplin: College Press, 2000). This is a commentary of some length, written by a scholar who spent his career as a Pepperdine University professor. His ties are with Churches of Christ. Womack has depended upon good authors and provides considerable background information.

Woods, Guy N., *A Commentary on the New Testament Epistles of Peter, John, and Jude*, (Nashville: Gospel Advocate, 1968). Guy N. Woods was a Churches of Christ preacher who published some of the commentaries in the Gospel Advocate New Testament series. He offers helpful outlines and good homiletical suggestions upon the text.

about the author

Thomas H. Olbricht grew up in Thayer, Missouri. He attended Harding University, Northern Illinois University, The University of Iowa and Harvard Divinity School. He studied Scripture, communication, and church history. He has taught at Harding University, The University of Dubuque and its Theological Seminary, The Pennsylvania State University, Abilene Christian University, and is Distinguished Professor Emeritus of Religion at Pepperdine University.

He has authored or edited nineteen books along with numerous essays in books and in periodicals. Along the way he has served as minister in several Churches of Christ, and has preached or lectured on every continent except for Antarctica.

He lives in retirement in South Berwick, Maine, along with his wife Dorothy. They have been married for fifty-four years and have five children and twelve grandchildren.